ALL THAT I HAVE IS YOURS

100 Meditations with St. Pope Kyrillos VI on the Spiritual Life

FATHER KYRILLOS IBRAHIM

ALL THAT I HAVE IS YOURS:
100 Meditations with St. Pope Kyrillos VI on the Spiritual Life

Published by:

ACTS Press
P.O. Box 4422
Anaheim, CA 92803

A Division of the Department of Christian Education within the Coptic Orthodox Diocese of Los Angeles, Southern California, and Hawaii

ISBN: 978-1-940661-18-6

Printed in the United States of America

"And he said to him, 'Son, you are always with me, and all that I have is yours'" (Lk 15:31).

"God ardently desires to see man ascend from strength to strength, from glory to glory, and cannot bear to see in him anything inferior to Himself. He bestows upon us all that is His: 'All that I have is yours.' Such is His will for us, and if we obey it, we will never be satisfied with ourselves, but always long to draw nearer to Him in hunger and thirst for the righteousness of God. Whosoever prepares his heart for this dynamic increase in Christ will continuously see 'greater things' in accordance with the Lord's promise."

(Zacharias Zacharou, *Remember Thy First Love*, p. 86)

CONTENTS

THE MIDNIGHT HOUR 169

Tribute to St. Pope Kyrillos VI

In the eyes of many men, you did not deserve the dignity of the papacy, having received the lowest number of votes. But in the eyes of God, you were the chosen one, the beloved of generations past and to come.

In the eyes of many men, you were considered ignorant at best, and at worst, a sorcerer and charlatan. But in the eyes of God, you were the living Gospel and the ambassador of His power and strength among a weak generation.

In the eyes of many men, you wasted your time in repetitive praises, empty liturgical rites, and desert escapism. But in the eyes of God, you knew how to secretly and quietly procure divine grace from all its hidden sources.

In the eyes of many men, you lacked the human capacity for planning, organizing, and managing the Church's affairs. But in the eyes of God, by your limitless humility, you provoked Him to act in your stead, accomplishing what was impossible by mere human effort.

In the eyes of many men, you relied on superstitious invocations of saints and angels as a deflection of your own insufficiency. But in the eyes of God, you were the beloved of those in Heaven, and they eagerly supported and defended their friend.

In the eyes of many men, you mumbled repetitious prayers from ancient texts and anointed with oil the sick who were desperate for more modern solutions. But in the eyes of God, your prayers called down fire from heaven, healing the body and the soul, changing hearts, and inflaming a hopeless generation with zeal and love for God and His Church.

In the eyes of many men, you died like all men die, confirming the vanity and futility of earthly life. But in the eyes of God, your death was the moment of a new, truer, and more potent life, an eternal partnership with Him Who makes all things new.

Biographical Timeline

- **August 2, 1902** - Birth of Azer Youssef Atta (future St. Pope Kyrillos VI) in Damanhur
- **July 27, 1927** - Azer enters El Baramous Monastery
- **February 25, 1928** - Azer ordained Monk with the name "Mina el-Baramousy"
- **July 18, 1931** - Monk Mina ordained a priest and begins at Helwan Theological Seminary
- **1933** - Pope Youannis XIX attempts to ordain Fr. Mina as Bishop. Fr. Mina flees to the St. Shenouda Monastery. Later that year, he returns to El Baramous Monastery
- **1934** - Begins his life in solitude in a desert cave a few miles outside of El Baramous
- **April 4, 1936** - Leaves his solitude and accompanies the expelled seven monks to Cairo
- **June 23, 1936** - Inhabits an abandoned windmill at Mokattam on the outskirts of Cairo
- **October 28, 1941** - Evicted from the Windmill for the first time by the Department of Egyptian Antiquities and lives between Old Cairo churches
- **December 1943** - Appointed Abbot of St. Samuel Monastery

- **March 16, 1945** - Elevated to the priestly rank of Hegumen by Metropolitan Athanasius. The same year, he leaves the St. Samuel Monastery and returns to the Windmill. He is evicted by the British a few months later and lives once again between Old Cairo churches
- **September 1947** - Fr. Mina establishes St. Mina's church in Old Cairo
- **1949** - Fr. Mina establishes a hostel for university students next to St Mina's Church in Old Cairo
- **May 10, 1959** - Father Mina is consecrated patriarch as H.H. Pope Kyrillos VI
- **June 22, 1959** - Consecrates St. Mina Monastery in Mariut
- **November 27, 1959** - Lays Foundation stone of St. Mina Monastery
- **July 24, 1965** - Lays foundation stone of new St. Mark's Cathedral in Cairo
- **April 2, 1968** - Holy Virgin Mary appears in Zeitoun
- **June 23, 1968** - Reception of St. Mark's relics from the Vatican
- **March 7, 1971** - Celebrates his last Divine Liturgy
- **March 9, 1971** - Repose of Pope Kyrillos VI
- **November 22, 1972** - Pope Kyrillos' body relocated to St. Mina Monastery in Mariut
- **June 20, 2013** - Canonized by the Holy Synod of the Coptic Orthodox Church, 42 years after his repose

Foreword

The life and example of St. Pope Kyrillos VI teaches us that God dwells in His saints at all times and in every place. Holiness is not limited to a certain time. St. Pope Kyrillos VI lived in the 20th century with all its developments and changes in society, but he gave us a model of the life of holiness, whether in his childhood, youth, or monastic life as a hermit. In his life as Patriarch, he shepherded the Church wisely and spiritually amid many difficulties.

St. Pope Kyrillos VI also teaches us that the most powerful weapon to face problems and hardships is the weapon of prayer. Prayer, as the Saint used to say, "moves mountains." He faced difficulties in his monastic life, so he left his monastery and lived from one place to another. As Patriarch, he faced problems from inside and out, but he faced them with prayer. God granted him to witness the Church during his papacy as She moved from glory to glory, whether in spiritual growth, educational advancement, monastic revival, construction of churches, or Her relationship with the government. Heaven showed its joy in this great saint through the apparition of the Holy Virgin Mary in a unique and unprecedented way.

Finally, the life of St. Pope Kyrillos VI shows us that the life of holiness has the greatest influence. St. Pope Kyrillos did not travel much and was not a preacher who had recorded sermons or books. But the depth of his influence on the souls of people whether in Egypt or outside Egypt, among the children of the Church or outside the Church, is a great testament of his holiness extending until now, fifty years since his departure.

We continue to feel his presence with us in the fragrance of holiness that permeates these pages.

Metropolitan Serapion

PREFACE

Today at ACTS Press we have the joy and privilege to publish this book that was several years in the making. For 50 years, readers of Arabic have had the privilege to access to the life, personality, and impact of St. Pope Kyrillos VI. Its publication opens the floodgates for English readers to one of our great saints, most recently canonized by the Coptic Orthodox Holy Synod on June 20, 2013. This publication is not only fortuitous on the 50th anniversary of his departure, but heavenly planned and executed beyond our expectations and abilities. For several years, Fr. Kyrillos Ibrahim has been compiling these stories of the blessed saint, along with his own meditations on the spiritual life with the Holy Trinity. The breadth and depth of the impact of these stories precipitated this publication. I firmly believe this work will provide abundant fruit in the lives of each who imbibe the fragrance of holiness from its pages.

We hope and pray that God would accept this offering–of Fr. Kyrillos Ibrahim, and all the servants who diligently and vigilantly labored night and day to complete this publication in due time–as a first-fruit for spiritual publications that will impart grace to our readers toward their edification. As the Saint advised one of his spiritual children, "Persist in and honor reading, if possible more than prayer. Reading is the spring of intelligent prayer. For, as I had previously told you, reading for a good purpose will show you how to walk on the virtuous path. Whoever reads the books to understand the path of virtue, this path will be opened before him."

May God allow that this publication and others open wide the glorious path of virtue to edification, sanctification, and glorification with the saints in the bosom of our beloved Lord.

Bishop Kyrillos

Introduction

The study of spirituality is an expedition into the lives of men and women who lived exceptional lives under the influence of the Holy Spirit. In our Orthodox tradition, the designation of who a saint is includes "the patriarchs, the prophets, the apostles, the preachers, the evangelists, the martyrs, the confessors and all the spirits of the righteous perfected in the Faith" (*Divine Liturgy of St. Basil*). In a real sense, they lived the Holy Scriptures and became an incarnation of the life of perfection. We might say that the saint is a perpetuation of the life of Christ in every generation. By studying their lives, we come to know Christ.

Utilizing the lives and writings of the saints, many have attempted to develop systematic manuals on spirituality, constructing the principles of the spiritual life and its development and advancement. In the East, most well-known, perhaps, is the *Ladder of Divine Ascent* by St. John Climacus. Though popularized among lay people in recent years, it was originally written by a hermit for other monks in solitary life. In it, he portrays the advancement of spiritual life as a ladder stretching from earth to heaven, consisting of thirty steps leading to union with God. Each step represents the spiritual struggle in terms of virtues and passions. Other expositions of the spiritual life were framed within three pronounced stages: purification (purgative), illumination (illuminative), and deification (unitive).

This book, however, is not intended to be a manual or a comprehensive explanation of advancing through stages in the spiritual life. Rather, the purpose of these brief meditations is to produce a broader panoramic view of the spiritual life like points on a sphere, where the sphere is the life of God. They are intended to encourage reflection and prayer, as well as inspire a greater commitment to a life of faith, hope, and love.

All That I Have is Yours

I would like to say a word on why I chose this title for the book. So often we think of the spiritual life in terms of "What must I do to inherit eternal life?" (Mk 10:17). Viewed from such a perspective, spirituality runs the risk of being reduced to another expression of the Law, a means of earning our way to perfection (Ga 2:21). A "still more excellent way" (1 Co 12:31) is divulged in the intimate conversation of the Lord Jesus with the Samaritan woman. Jesus spoke of Himself to her as "the gift of God" (Jn 4:10). A gift cannot be earned; it can only be received. This revelation indicates a shift in orientation; spiritual life is primarily about what God wants to do in us. Our cooperation with God's grace is about attaining greater receptivity and capacity for God's life and gifts.

More forcefully, turning to the Parable of the Prodigal Son (Lk 15:11-31), we discover within the drama that both sons miss the mark of the true nature of their father. The final word of the father is a staggering revelation of God and a paramount message of our salvation: "Son, you are always with me, and all that I have is yours" (Lk 15:31). God is self-gift. Only when we come to truly perceive the immense generosity of God's love and His eagerness to give us "all that He has," can we also respond in a self-gift of ourselves, both to Him and to our neighbor. As St. John the Evangelist says, "We love Him because He first loved us" (1 Jn 4:19). Spiritual life, then, is first receptivity, and then reciprocity.

St. Pope Kyrillos VI

The stories presented in this book surrounding the life of one of the greatest modern saints, St. Pope Kyrillos VI, are not intended to be a display of astonishing miracles; they are about encounters. Through these encounters, we discover the Saint who became a self-gift to his people, both Christian and non-Christian.

I recall over thirty years ago asking my spiritual father–who knew the Saint and served alongside him for almost ten years–what was the secret, the key, to the mystery of St. Pope Kyrillos' sanctity. His answer came quick, without a hesitation—he was a beggar! As he said this, he motioned with his hands the gesture of one begging with open palms. Thirty years later, I still haven't come across a better description.

"Blessed are the poor in spirit, for theirs is the kingdom of heaven" (Mt 5:3). Completely emptied of himself, he was purely receptive to the Divine life and God's gifts.

Although we cannot imitate him as a miracle-worker, we are certainly called to follow his example of love, kindness, generosity, forgiveness, and humility. Moreover, his attentiveness to his own spiritual life, especially the life of prayer, worship, and asceticism points to the storehouses of grace that exist in the Church for all of us, since we are all nourished with the same milk and from the same Mother. In another sense, these encounters are reminders for us to take seriously our own contact with the Lord. God's grace is abundantly poured out to those who desire Him with all their heart. "Ask, and it will be given you; seek, and you will find; knock, and it will be opened to you" (Mt 7:7).

How to Use This Book

The book consists of approximately 100 chapters, each consisting of three distinct entries: a psalm verse, a story of a real encounter with St. Pope Kyrillos VI, and a spiritual meditation. The three entries are not intended to be connected by a common theme. Instead, they are independent reflections to assist you in prayer and conversion of life. You might look at them as a three-course meal.

We need to discover our "deep heart" (Ps 63:6). Spiritual masters have described prayer as the descent of the mind into the heart. Simply stated, reading a spiritual text or prayer first begins in the mind. But it must not remain there; it ought to enter into the heart. We can ascertain that the mind entered the heart if we are roused to contrition, gratitude, humility, faith, hope, or love. Then we know that the heart has been "activated" and we learn to live from the heart.

The structure of the book is centered around the Coptic Orthodox *Agpeya* (Book of Hours). It begins with the introductory psalm (Psalm 50) and then moves through all the canonical hours beginning with the First Hour through the Midnight Hour. For the Midnight Hour, I used only Psalm 118 divided into its twenty-two stanzas from the First Watch, since the remaining Psalms are included in earlier Hours.

For each Psalm, I selected a single verse that can be reflected on, memorized, and used as an arrow prayer. Of course, according to one's circumstances, it is good to pray the full Psalm. The goal is to progress, more generally, in praying the Psalms and to encourage, more specifically, the use of the *Agpeya*.

Next are the stories from the life and encounters with our beloved saint, St. Pope Kyrillos VI. I am certain that these stories will move you, not only to love him more and seek his intercession, but to follow him, for he is indeed a trustworthy guide. I believe that he says to us today, "Imitate me, just as I also imitate Christ." (1 Co 11:1)

Lastly are the spiritual meditations which cover a wide range of reflections on the spiritual life. I have attempted to touch on different subjects, themes, and considerations in the spiritual life without being repetitive. I hope that they will ultimately inspire you to go deeper in spiritual reading.

A final note on the numbering of the Psalms: for the Psalm verses, I used the Septuagint/Coptic numbering along with the Masoretic numbering in parentheses. The numbering of the Psalms within the spiritual meditations follow the Septuagint rendering.

Fr. Kyrillos Ibrahim

March 9, 2021

On the occasion of the 50th Anniversary of the Departure of St. Pope Kyrillos VI

Introductory Psalm

PSALM 50 (51)

"Restore to me the joy of Your salvation"

St. Pope Kyrillos VI used to visit St. Mina's Church in Old Cairo from time to time. One day, on his way back to his residence, he noticed a crying child in the distance. The child worked in his brother Michael's house. After the Pope arrived at the Patriarchate, he called his brother to inquire why the child was crying, fearing that someone had insulted her. He found out that the children in the neighborhood had called her "servant" in a derogatory fashion.

The Saint was emotionally moved and sent his driver to bring her to his residence. When she arrived, he talked to her full of kindness and gave her an autographed bill of money to cherish as a blessing. To lift her spirits, he told her that, from now on, she should say that she was serving the Pope of Alexandria. She left delighted and always remembered that event.

On another occasion, there was a church trip that came by bus to visit St. Pope Kyrillos VI in one of the churches he was visiting. When they arrived, one of the elderly ladies felt too weak to enter due to her health and the crowds. She decided to stay on the bus while the rest of the group went in and joined the crowds of people to receive the blessing of the Saint. When one of the servants from that trip reached His Holiness to take his blessing, the Pope surprised him by asking him to go back to the bus and to tell the elderly lady to come in because the Pope has a special seat for her right next to him.

On Divine Filiation

So much of our earthly life is spent trying to figure out, and then live, a human vocation—something that gives meaning, purpose and direction to my life. The word "vocation" from the Latin *vocatio,* and its equivalent in Greek, *klisi,* do not connote simply a choice or a preference, but literally means a "calling" or a "summons." What is it that we have been summoned to? The Gospel according to St. John begins by pointing to what our Lord brought to humanity: "But as many as received Him, to them He gave the right to become children of God, to those who believe in His name" (Jn 1:11-13). After his conversion, St. Paul the Apostle, came to experience this radical vocation, a significant shift from his previous understanding of living according to the Law to the life of Grace through adoption. "For all who are led by the Spirit of God are sons of God. For you did not receive the spirit of slavery to fall back into fear, but you have received the Spirit of adoption as sons, by whom we cry, 'Abba! Father!'" (Ro 8:14).

Man's first and truest vocation is divine sonship, our adoption as children in Christ. Anyone who does not realize that he is a child of God is unaware of the deepest truth about himself. Sin does not change this from God's perspective as the Prodigal Son learned; it only confuses the sinner who forgets and tries to renounce this filiation. This divine sonship is not only the fundamental status of a Christian, which should pervade our every action and motive, but the secure source of our joy. Joy arises from the possession, or the hope of possessing, a good. And sadness comes from losing, or the fear of losing, a good. There can be no greater good than our divine filiation.

If we build our joy and hope on temporal earthly things like health, beauty, pleasure, professional success, and so on, even in the best circumstances we will eventually become unsatisfied and lack true joy. Always remember that your true identity and vocation are that you have become "fellow citizens with the saints and members of the household of God" (Eph 2:19).

THE FIRST HOUR

PSALM 1

"For the Lord knows the way of the righteous"

In 1962, a certain lady who worked as a school teacher was transferred to a new position in Cairo. She used to go regularly to the cathedral early in the morning where the Pope was praying and attend the Morning Raising of Incense and the Divine Liturgy before going to work.

In 1964, she started experiencing many problems from some malicious people at work. It became likely that she would be unjustly penalized. She decided to write the entire problem on a piece of paper and went to see St. Pope Kyrillos VI at the cathedral in order to ask for his prayers.

She was holding the note in her left hand behind her back and waited for the Pope at the bottom of the stairway of his residence, at the time he usually came down to enter the Cathedral. As soon as the Saint saw her, he smiled, moved his papal staff from his right hand to his left, then pulled her left hand out from behind her back with his right hand. Before she could say anything, he took the note and told her, "Go to work and do not fear anything. The Lord is with you!"

That same week she was found innocent and nothing negative befell her at all.

On the Virtue of Faith

Faith can be understood in terms of both dogmatic theology and spiritual theology. When we speak of the "contents of faith," we usually mean dogmatic theology and what the Church teaches in its definitions of faith relating to the Holy Trinity or Christology and so on. But in spiritual theology, faith is a virtue, an attitude and a way of life in a personal relationship with the Living God. It means that faith can never be an intellectual activity of assent, but a life steeped in growing trust, hope, obedience, and abandonment. Faith is both a gift from God and the foundation upon which everything in the spiritual life is built.

Faith is a constant impulse of the divine life in the human soul. Whenever there is faith, there is a real and direct encounter with God. The gift of faith is given by God to all, but the contents of faith are transmitted through the Church. Like every gift of God, it has the potential to grow and expand or to wane and atrophy. This is what Jesus spoke of when He said, "For whoever has, to him more will be given, and he will have abundance; but whoever does not have, even what he has will be taken away from him" (Mt 13:12). We might say that this is a spiritual law not unlike other natural laws that exist in the world. For example, if I lift weights properly, I will increase my muscle mass. If I stop lifting weights, I won't simply stop progressing, but I will lose even the muscle mass I acquired, and it is quite possible that I end up in a worse position than the one I started with. Faith is the same way—we must never stop acquiring, utilizing and employing the gift of faith. The question remains, how can we grow in faith? Faith can be viewed from three dimensions or sources: faith that comes through the witness of others, faith that expands through our own experiences, and faith received as an infusion of God's grace to the soul through our obedience and cooperation.

PSALM 2

"Blessed are all who take refuge in Him"

In Alexandria, there happened to be a two-year-old child who contracted acute pneumonia. His parents became very distressed, especially as he was their only child after eight years of marriage and a struggle to have children. When they took him to the doctor, he didn't give them any hope and they wept bitterly.

His father remembered that St. Pope Kyrillos VI happened to be there in Alexandria. He was determined to see the Saint no matter how late it was. The parents took their son and arrived at the Patriarchate very late at night. In spite of their tears, the guard refused to let them in. However, the Pope, who was in prayer at that time, knew by the Spirit what was happening outside. He called the guard and said to him, "Let them in, their son is sick."

The daring parents went inside crying and, before anyone explained anything to him, the Saint immediately placed the Cross on the spot where the pain was. He prayed and told them, "Don't worry, the Lord will bless him." The parents went home with profound peace and the child's condition immediately began to improve. The next day, they took him to the doctor, and after examining the child, he smiled in astonishment and said, "Good news! Your son had pneumonia, but now there is no trace of the disease."

On the Witness of Faith

It can be said that we "catch" faith from others. That is, through the mystery of our Christian fraternity, the witness of someone else's faith can be transmitted to me and become in me an impulse to a greater movement of faith in my own life. In the prologue of St. John the Evangelist's first epistle, the Apostle sets out to communicate to an early Christian community the joy of faith that is rightfully theirs due to the experience of the disciples, whom they have come to trust:

> ...which we have heard, which we have seen with our eyes, which we have looked upon, and our hands have handled, concerning the Word of life...that which we have seen and heard we declare to you, that you also may have fellowship with us...that your joy may be full (1 Jn 1:1, 3, 4).

Faith is a movement of God's life toward man and this movement can be direct and also indirect through others. When Christ showed Himself to St. Thomas after the Resurrection, not only was Thomas' faith made whole, but so also was ours. When Christ opened the eyes of the blind man, we also received the light of faith. Here we see the intrinsic relationship between reading the Holy Scriptures, the lives of the saints and even reading the imprint of the Creator on creation as powerful witnesses to the manifestation of God leading us to faith.

Paradoxically, in the New Testament, the manifestation of God is not principally in mighty deeds and miracles, but through the Passion and the Cross, where Divine Love reaches its summit. Jesus said, "And I, if I am lifted up from the earth, will draw all peoples to Myself" (Jn 12:32). Thus, in Christian life, the Cross is not only a foundation but a signpost. That is why often the greatest witness of faith is the suffering and death of a believer in union with Christ. To see someone suffering who is nonetheless joyful, peaceful, and grateful to God is a divine encounter leading us to faith. And if it's possible to "catch" faith from others, it is likewise our mission to "throw" faith in the direction of others through the power of our own union with Jesus.

PSALM 3

"With my voice I cried unto the Lord and He heard me"

In 1963, Gamal suffered severe dermatitis in a very sensitive area which the doctors diagnosed as an allergy. He was bedridden for fifty days because the inflammation caused skin ulcers and he couldn't wear any clothes. Many dermatologists saw him, prescribing a variety of medications, but to no avail.

One day a friend visited him and gave him a piece of the holy bread (*antidoron* or *baraka* or *eulogia*) and said, "Pope Kyrillos is now in Alexandria, go receive his blessing!" He went to the Patriarchate the same day; it was about 5:30 p.m. When he asked to see the Pope, he was told that His Holiness would not see anyone that evening because he had a long tiresome day and already retired to his residence. Gamal did not give up hope and sat down next to His Holiness' brother, Hanna. That evening saw many people come and go but Gamal stayed until 9:30 p.m. At that moment, the telephone rang in an adjoining room. Hanna took the call...it was the Pope who said to his brother, "Is there a person named Gamal there? St. Mina woke me up from my sleep and told me that Gamal was waiting outside to see me. Let him in."

Hanna returned quickly and asked the man, "Is your name Gamal?" When he answered him affirmatively, he added, "His Holiness wants to see you," and told him about the phone call. As the man entered, they brought a glass of water to His Holiness who made the sign of the Cross and breathed on it. He then drank half the water and gave Gamal the rest to drink. He also gave him a little bottle of holy oil, and asked him to rub the affected area for three consecutive nights after which he would be cured. The man left joyful and did as he was told. On the morning of the fourth day, the infections and ulcers were completely gone.

On the Experience of Faith

Just as the disciples in the Gospel encountered crises of faith on numerous occasions, so each one of us, as long as we are in the flesh, will encounter trials of faith until the last moments of our lives. And just as the disciples grew from their experiences, so also for us the trials and difficulties of faith we encounter can be experiences of transformation leading us from faith to greater faith. "Lord, I believe; help my unbelief!" (Mk 9:24).

In the experience of the disciples caught in the storm (Mt 14:22-32), what amazes us is not so much that the disciples might have wavered in their faith from fear, but that such hesitation to trust God came immediately after they themselves participated in the great miracle of feeding the multitudes (Mt 14:13-18). This quivering of faith is often mirrored in our own lives when we forget God's presence in our past. We need to keep a sort of "inventory" of our past trials remembering God's saving actions or the good that came out of our difficulties even if they had not turned out the way we initially had hoped for.

Faith needs to be stretched and even torn at times in order to grow and soar, very much like a muscle must be stretched and torn in order that, through its healing, it grows bigger and stronger. That means at times enduring the painful experiences of darkness, insecurity, mystery, and the incomprehensibility of God's judgments and ways. Faith must pass through the darkness of the mind, the senses, the emotions, and even to the abyss of abandonment. "My God, My God, why have You forsaken Me?" (Mt 27:46; Ps 21:1).

When the light of God's presence shines in the darkness of the trials of faith, this light will begin to illuminate our thoughts, perspectives, interpretations, and appraisals of everything happening around us and within us. Moving forward, everything will speak to us of God, will become a sign of His presence, and will draw us toward Him.

PSALM 4

"You have given gladness to my heart"

A newly-ordained priest was asked by St. Pope Kyrillos VI to celebrate Vespers in a church located in a remote area of Cairo which was still being built. There was great difficulty in reaching the church, especially since he did not own a car and would have to walk for a long time in difficult conditions. The priest took his son with him to assist in the service.

The next day, the priest went to His Holiness and before he could say anything, the Pope said to him, "My son, go and raise incense for Vespers on Thursday in the same place again." When the Pope saw his hesitation (since it was both difficult to travel there and no one was even attending services at this church), he said again, "My son, go and raise incense for Vespers so that you may attain a blessing."

The priest went, again taking his son with him. As he began celebrating the Vespers, he descended from the Holy Sanctuary to offer incense toward the Royal Door and was astonished to find the first five rows of pews filled with holy Anchorite Fathers (the "spirit-borne" or *sowah,* which is literally "sojourner" or "traveler" in Arabic). Even more, he saw that the Pope himself was there amongst them. The priest was overwhelmingly consoled by this spiritual vision. He completed the prayers and at the end of the service he did not find any of the Anchorite Fathers remaining. But what happened next was even more wonderful! As he was leaving with his son, he saw a great vision of Archangel Michael surrounded by a great heavenly light and who seemed very pleased.

The priest, completely overjoyed, rushed straight to meet the Pope at St. Mark's Cathedral in Cairo. As he was about to tell him what he saw, he found the Saint sitting and surrounded by a divine light. The Saint looked at the priest with a smile and said in a loving and fatherly tone, "You see, my son, the blessings which you received today? And did you see me there?" He answered, "I saw you there, *Sayedna* ("Our Master"), with the Holy Anchorite Fathers in the Church!" The Saint looked at him with a smile and gave him his blessing. The priest was filled with joy at the magnificent beauty of the Church as well as the extraordinary spirituality of St. Pope Kyrillos VI.

On the Obedience of Faith

God initiates every creative, redemptive and salvific act in man's life. The first impulse to faith is a divine gift. But once the supernatural life is set in motion, faith needs a response that allows it to grow and be nurtured so as to lead us to total abandonment to God. We can speak of an "obedience of faith" which represents a synergy between God's grace and man's free will.

In the Sermon on the Mount, the Lord Jesus gave a series of commandments, precepts, and instructions covering prayer, fasting, almsgiving, ways of dealing with our enemies and many other topics. We could say that the whole of the sermon presents each one of us with the possibility of obeying or disobeying the Divine Law on things that impact our religious, familial, and social lives. At the end of the sermon, Jesus concludes with the consequences of our obedience or disobedience:

> 'Therefore whoever hears these sayings of Mine, and does them, I will liken him to a wise man who built his house on the rock: and the rain descended, the floods came, and the winds blew and beat on that house; and it did not fall, for it was founded on the rock. But everyone who hears these sayings of Mine, and does not do them, will be like a foolish man who built his house on the sand: and the rain descended, the floods came, and the winds blew and beat on that house; and it fell. And great was its fall.' And so it was, when Jesus had ended these sayings, that the people were astonished at His teaching (Mt 7:24-28).

The Lord connects obedience with an increase in faith at the time a trial comes, and disobedience with our failure to believe, trust, and endure at the time of trial. Thus, we might deduce that the divine and free gift of faith is given to those who through obedience are "faithful." When you are faithful to the commandments, to the duties of your God-inspired vocation, to the teachings and disciplines of the Church, and to every other divine authority, then you are preparing yourself for a greater infusion of faith.

PSALM 5

"Lead me in Your ways of righteousness, O Lord"

During a visit of St. Pope Kyrillos VI to Lower Egypt, in the town of Desouq, a great tent was set up to welcome him in which many political and religious leaders were there to greet him.

During the welcome of His Holiness, a tall man, who was not Christian, approached and was about to hug the Pope to take his blessing. But the Saint rebuked him saying, "What is this?! You smell bad!" The man walked away in shock from what happened and kept thinking, "What does he mean by 'I smell bad?'"

The man then remembered that he had placed some illegal drugs in his pocket. He removed the drugs and went in again in a second attempt to greet the Pope and receive his blessing. This time, the Saint smiled at him and said, "This is better! Now you smell nice! Go, my son, may God protect you!"

The man returned home, but before he entered his house, the police were there to arrest him. They searched him carefully, expecting to find the drugs in his possession, but didn't find anything. The man smiled to himself and said, "Now I smell nice," and " God protects me," just as the Pope said!

Another time, a deacon was assisting at the early morning Divine Liturgy with St. Pope Kyrillos VI. He was approached by another deacon who asked him, "Do you see anything in my pockets?" It was a strange question so he responded, "I don't understand what you mean."

Again he asked, "Is there anything about my appearance that attracts your attention? Do you see anything in my pockets?"

"No, nothing. I can't see anything."

"Then why did Pope Kyrillos ask me to leave what was in my pockets outside of the church before he would allow me to join in the prayers?"

"You must certainly be carrying something in there."

"I am carrying a gun... here it is... But you couldn't see it so how did the Pope know what I was carrying?"

On God's Search for Man

Before entering the home of Zacchaeus the Tax Collector (Lk 19:1-10), Jesus told the Parable of the Lost Sheep to those who objected to Him making company with sinners. In the parable, the Shepherd Himself goes out in search of one lost sheep. We all know that anxious feeling of searching for something we have lost that is precious and valuable to us. Likewise, God's search for man, who is the pinnacle of His creative love, has been echoed since the beginning after Adam's Fall when the voice of God first resounded to all of humanity crying out, "Where are you?" (Ge 3:9).

God's search for you is personal: "I have redeemed you; I have called you by your name; You are Mine" (Is 43:1). No soul is like another, and in God's eyes, each soul is uniquely the object of His creative, redemptive, and salvific love. Many Fathers and saints of the Church have echoed this truth–that the Incarnation, Passion, Death, and Resurrection of Christ would have taken place if you were the only one who had sinned and been in need of redemption.

The Christian life is not so much about our effort to find God but to allow ourselves to be found by God Who is searching for us and pleased to grant us all that is His (Lk 15:31). "You did not choose Me, but I chose you" (Jn 15:16). Perhaps the reason we miss the visitation of the Lord is simply because we are distracted, focused on too many temporal and corruptible priorities. It could be that we have not yet realized the dissatisfaction that life apart from God eventually brings. Or maybe, like much of the crowd following Jesus through the streets of Jericho, we are simply "curious" about religion, spirituality, and the question of God.

Curiosity is not the same as desire. True desire will pay any price to obtain the object of its desire. Curiosity is like an itch to know, and it makes for entertaining debates in the halls of college campuses, but curiosity does not have the will to act. "Blessed are those who hunger and thirst for righteousness, for they shall be filled" (Mt 5:6). The hungry are in search of crumbs and have their hands extended, vigilant, and ready to receive.

PSALM 6

"I am exhausted from my sighing, every night I flood my bed with my tears"

A long-time acquaintance of St. Pope Kyrillos VI was accustomed to always celebrating the Feast of St Mina (that falls on June 22) at his monastery in Mariut. In 1967, during the Six-Day War between Egypt and Israel, he was arrested and placed in a detention center, a place notorious for torture. For eleven days he never stopped crying out, "St Mina! St. Mina! I am innocent! I am innocent!"

Amazingly, on June 22, he was the only prisoner released from the detention center. The next day he went to see St. Pope Kyrillos VI, barely able to walk from the physical torture they inflicted upon him. When St. Pope Kyrillos saw him, he said to him, "Are you angry with St. Mina?" He responded, "No, Your Holiness." The Pope explained, "St. Mina said not to be upset with him. He came and asked me to tell you not to be upset with him. He said that you called out to him numerous times but because of all his sons in trouble at Sinai that needed his help to save their lives, he needed to attend to them, but he preserved your life and bones unbroken."

He showed the Pope his mutilated back, "How do you like this?!" His back was full of cavities from the flesh being torn out. It was such a painful scene that the Saint began to weep, his tears wetting his beard.

The Pope went and brought holy oil from the vigil lamp burning in front of St. Mina's icon. He began praying and rubbing his back with the oil. From his crying you couldn't understand the words he was saying. He did that for half an hour then said, "Here you go, St. Mina kept his promise, go look in the mirror." The man was stunned to see that the flesh which had fallen off his back came back and the cavities were filled and even every scratch was gone.

On the Virtue of Hope

St. Paul calls hope an "anchor of the soul" (Heb 6:19). Just as an anchor keeps a ship firmly in place preventing it from being tossed or smashed against the rocks by the pressure of the current or winds, so hope is the virtue that provides stability, peace, and even joy in the midst of trials, difficulties, and confusions. Hope is rooted and established in Who God is, not in the possibilities or outcomes of the situations themselves.

Therein lies a crucial distinction between Christian hope and optimism. Whereas optimism tries to minimize the darkness, to see the glass half-full rather than half-empty, hope fully acknowledges the darkness and the evil, but rests in God's presence and His faithful promises. In fact–and this is certainly the witness of many saints–it is precisely in those times of darkness that we can become aware of God's presence as a burst of Divine Light overwhelming us with a heavenly joy that surpasses any earthly peace or happiness we seek.

Hope, then, does not grant any assurance of a painless life, but rather acknowledges the presence of Him Who accompanies us in the midst of the pain–a presence that brings light, peace, and joy. Hope's fulfillment is in possession, which will only be completely realized in the Kingdom of God. There, we will no longer need the virtue of hope, for we shall possess all that we hoped for. But the seed of that possession is already implanted in us through our baptism, and it is nourished and finds its growth through prayer, spiritual reading, the Mysteries (Sacraments), and worship—all of which aim to arouse His presence within our hearts.

Hope is not only forward-looking. As we come to experience in greater depths and degrees the presence of God and the joy this brings, we not only grow in anticipation of our future possession, but we also look back to our past with a greater awareness of God's presence in those moments that up to now have only brought us regret and shame. As such, hope is a powerful purification of our memories.

PSALM 8

"What is man that You are mindful of him?"

Mohammed, a non-Christian editor of a magazine in Alexandria, was at a meeting in 1970 at the Cathedral of St. Mark in Alexandria where St. Pope Kyrillos VI was present. The meeting was a planning session for an upcoming journalistic mission to Ethiopia.

During the meeting, one of the Pope's aides offered the guests some chocolates, but the man apologized for not taking any, because he was a diabetic and his insulin levels were very high. His Holiness insisted that he take one, and after a few moments he insisted that he take another one. Before he left, the Saint placed his hand on his head, prayed then said, "Mohammed, you are no longer diabetic."

After Ethiopia, he went on another mission in Lebanon. He forgot everything that the Pope told him and was still under the assumption that he was diabetic. While in Lebanon, he found it very difficult to stick to his diet but resolved to go on a strict diet once returning to Egypt.

After he returned to Alexandria, he had a full test done by a pathologist and the results showed a lower than normal level of insulin. He still did not remember what the Pope had told him. He met with the Professor of Internal Diseases at Alexandria University to get an assessment of these results, which he doubted. To his amazement, the doctor stated that he was cured and insisted on knowing how it had happened. It was only then that he remembered what had happened when he met St. Pope Kyrillos VI.

On God's Bountiful Love

The Parable of the Sower (Mt 13:1-9) depicts the simple image of a farmer who goes out to sow his seed anticipating and hoping for a fruitful harvest. Jesus uses this imagery to tell us about God the Father. While it is certainly true that an important aspect of the parable is an emphasis on the different kinds of soil and what they represent in terms of the human heart, as well as the seed that is sown, we should not pass over an obvious flaw in the farmer himself.

It would be supposed that an experienced farmer would recognize which kinds of soil might be suitable for sowing seed with the potential of bringing forth fruit. There is a certain recklessness associated with farmer's actions—He throws the seeds everywhere, almost without discernment. But perhaps this is really the point of the parable: God's love is indulgent, seemingly reckless, and in His relentless pursuit of every human soul that He persists in throwing the seeds of His love, grace, and word until man has had every opportunity to receive it and be transformed by it. "Behold, I stand at the door and knock. If anyone hears My voice and opens the door, I will come in to him and dine with him, and he with Me" (Re 3:20). In this sense, we can interpret this parable in the light of the Parable of the Lost Coin (Lk 15:8-10). The woman who loses one of her ten silver coins spends the whole night persistently searching for it, and when she finds it, she spends the money celebrating with friends and family!

It seems our first concern in the description of the various kinds of soils should not be that we, in our presumption, might self-diagnose which category of soil we fall under. In reality, everything that is problematic in the bad soil types is the effect of sin in my life. Not to ignore human effort toward transformation, but to give the preeminence to God's generous and seemingly reckless love which persists, despite all that is sinful and miserable in me, to gradually make my heart a good soil yielding a crop thirty, sixty, and a hundredfold.

PSALM 11 (12)

"You, O Lord, will watch over us and preserve us from this generation"

A priest from Alexandria serving at a church in the name of St. Mina went to the Patriarchate in Cairo. When he met with St. Pope Kyrillos, the Pope asked him to go and pray the Vespers Raising of Incense in a church named after St. George. He did not have a car, so he took the bus which was crowded. Some thieves on the bus stole his watch and the silver hand Cross that he had prayed with.

When he got off the bus and realized that he lost the Cross and the watch, he was upset, and began to blame St. Mina, saying within himself, "How could St. Mina let those thieves steal the silver Cross that I use to pray with on the Altar consecrated after his name?"

The next day, he went to the Patriarchate and as soon as St. Pope Kyrillos saw him, the Pope laughed and said, "You got robbed and you asked St. Mina for the Cross. Why didn't you ask for the watch, too? St. Mina will only send you the Cross, because that's all you asked for!"

Two days later, while the priest was sitting outside in the courtyard of the church, a man came asking for him. The man took out the Cross from his pocket and said, "I'm a goldsmith and I make silver. A man came to me to sell this Cross but I knew it was stolen because your name is inscribed on it, so I bought it from him and I brought it to you." The priest asked the man, "Didn't he try to also sell you a watch?" The goldsmith laughed and said, "No, only the Cross." The priest lifted up his eyes and said, "St. Mina, I wish I would have asked you for the watch too!"

On the Goodness of God's Providence

There is much that can be known, though not easily followed, about the Will of God through the Holy Scriptures, the lives of the saints and the devotional life of the Church. We hear and read about the commandments and evangelical counsels as they relate to morality, worship, and Christian piety. But what about the things that happen to us that leave us confused and unsure, questioning their meaning and value, whether they are truly from God or not? St. Augustine tells us that though we do not always understand it, everything that appears to be random, chaotic, and without God's direction, takes place according to God's will.

Simply, we can categorize everything that happens and exists as either part of God's stated or signified Will, or His permissive or providential Will. This means that even evil, which can never be ascribed to God, is nonetheless permitted by Him and, therefore, part of His good providence. The key to accepting this peacefully and joyfully throughout our lives is by trust and confidence in the goodness of God. He would never allow the evil to exist or touch me unless He was both good enough and powerful enough to bring about a greater good than the evil itself. Jesus entreats us not to be afraid because the very hairs of our head are numbered (Lk 12:7). And, as the saints testify, the providence of God never sleeps!

For the soul that is completely abandoned to God, everything that we experience in every moment is a personal "word" of God to me and the best thing that can happen to me. Even my bad choices and my willful sins when placed in humble trust at the feet of Jesus are not a limitation for God's ability to bring about something beautiful and useful to my salvation, and even for benefit of others. They are like rotten manure which the Divine Farmer uses to make the earth produce abundant fruit.

What matters is not what I understand or perceive in the situation, but my confidence in God's goodness. Many saints have used the analogy of a needlepoint tapestry. The back of the frame appears to be a disorganized and chaotic mess. But the image that is rendered on the other side is the divine pattern.

PSALM 12 (13)

"How long will You hide Your face from me?"

For many years a man living in Cairo suffered from angina pectoris which caused him chest and back pain, and a heart arrhythmia. One day while in great pain he went to St. Mark's Cathedral to pray and there ran into his brother-in-law who loved St. Pope Kyrillos very much. He suggested they go to meet the Pope and receive his blessing. Vespers had just concluded and the congregation filled the reception hall of the Patriarchate waiting to receive His Holiness' blessing.

The man narrated what happened next:

"When we reached the Pope, my brother-in-law just pointed to me and Pope Kyrillos turned to him and said, 'Ok, my son.' His Holiness looked at me very intensely with a gaze that deeply pierced me within. At this point, His Holiness called one of the staff and asked him to escort me upstairs via the elevator, not the stairs. He asked me to wait there for him until he finished blessing the rest of the congregation.

"Surprisingly, he called me by my name and yet it was the first time I ever met His Holiness. My feet felt like they were nailed to the ground for two reasons: first, because he knew my name, and second, because he knew the nature of my illness as was clear by his asking me to take the elevator.

"I waited for His Holiness for some time and as soon as he saw me, he called me again by my name. I knelt and he placed his Cross on my heart and prayed ardently. He then called his private deacon and asked him to bring a piece of cotton soaked in holy oil. He instructed me to apply the holy oil where I felt the pain and said, 'I will send you St. Mina.'

"It was a long, long night, my heart roaring with pain. I felt like there was a ton of metal crushing my chest. I was suffocating and couldn't breathe. I could barely put the cotton of holy oil on my chest and couldn't even remove it, so I just left it there. I was so tired and I couldn't move. Around 3:00 a.m. I saw someone coming toward me, a shadow. He moved the piece of cotton around my chest. The load was suddenly lifted. My lungs opened up after feeling they had been closed for so long. I was finally able to take in a breath of fresh air. My heartbeat was also back to normal. 'It's a miracle!' I shouted. Then, shaking my wife vigorously, I said, 'I am healed, I can breathe normally and my heart is fine!'

"Thinking that I was delirious because of my high fever, my wife told me to make the sign of the Cross and go back to sleep.

"At 5:00 a.m., happy, awake, and energetic, I dressed quickly and took the first bus to the Patriarchate. The Pope was praying the early Divine Liturgy, which I attended. When the Pope came near me while carrying the censer, he whispered, 'I sent you St. Mina.' My heart was leaping with joy and full of gratitude. I answered, giving praise, 'St. Mina came to me and healed me, and I came early to show my gratitude and declare my faith. May the Lord grant Your Holiness a long life!'"

On Holy Waiting

The experience of waiting is often unpleasant. We do not particularly like waiting in traffic, waiting for our work day to end, waiting for our exam results, and so on. Human ingenuity and contemporary society continue to find ways to eliminate our need to wait. Fast-food and drive-thru restaurants, overnight home deliveries, faster computer processors, and telemedicine are all examples of useful progress. However, we must not lose our sense of waiting as a virtue related to patience, endurance, fortitude, and even joyful anticipation.

Throughout salvation history, waiting on God always meant preparation, anticipation and even conversion. The Israelites waited for forty years wandering in the desert before entering the Promised Land. Later, they waited seventy years in captivity before returning to their homeland. Of course, the Annunciation event recalls that the people of God were waiting thousands of years for the Messiah.

The Mother of God waited for the promise of the Child to be born of her; she waited throughout Jesus' ministry as God's plan unfolded; and she waited at the foot of the Cross for the world's redemption. All of this cost her much—a suffering unlike anyone else apart from her Son. And yet, this pain was accompanied by joyful anticipation and deep, interior peace. The Church, likewise, continues to wait for Her Bridegroom in His Second Coming, "looking" for the resurrection of the dead and the life of the coming age.

Waiting, therefore, is an essential element in the spiritual life. But it is not an empty waiting, because we know that God is present and fills every moment. The key is to let God give meaning to our waiting and not insist on our own expectations of how our waiting should be fulfilled. Fr. Henri Nouwen uses the expression "open-ended" waiting to express this idea that we must give up control of our future, letting God define, give meaning, and bring out good from it according to His love. "The Lord is good to those who wait for Him, to the soul who seeks Him" (La 3:25).

PSALM 14 (15)

"O Lord, who may dwell in Your sanctuary?"

In July 1958, a man was suffering from paralysis in the nerves of his right eye which caused him to have double vision. He was treated by several doctors including a well-known neurologist who treated him for eight months before some improvement.

In October 1961 the same disease came back. Disheartened, he went to the same specialist again and was advised to stop working and stay at home. At about 5:45 a.m. on a Tuesday morning in November 1961, the doorkeeper of the Holy Virgin Mary and Archangel Michael Church, which was adjacent to his house, knocked on his door and told him, "Go to the church, Pope Kyrillos VI is in the church now!"

He hurried to the church and attended the morning prayers with the Saint. After the service, he followed the Pope inside the Sanctuary and said to him, "Your Holiness, my eye is paralyzed!" The Saint asked him to take off his glasses. The Saint placed his hand Cross on his eye, prayed for several minutes, and then said, "By God's will, you will recover. Congratulations!" Within a week, he gained back his eyesight and stopped all treatments. The disease never returned.

On the Eucharist and Faith

A religion that does not manifest and bear witness to supernatural realities is reduced to a philosophy. A church that simply does good in this life, however noble, but does not give us an experience and taste of the mystical and supernatural life, has failed in its purpose and mission. In God's goodness, He sends to every generation authentic saints whose aim it is to awaken us to these spiritual realities often "in signs and wonders and mighty deeds" (2 Co 12:12). This is, then, one possible definition or role of the saint: to act as "prophet" to his or her generation.

Christ has bestowed upon His Church the mystery of God's plan, the "things which angels desire to look into" (1 Pe 1:12). Just before the distribution of Holy Communion, the celebrant priest recites an inaudible prayer connecting this verse to the Mystery of the Eucharist: "We give thanks to You, O Lord God the Almighty, for Your mercy is great upon us, for You have prepared for us those things which the angels desire to behold."

The Eucharist, like all the Mysteries (Sacraments), is a mystery of faith leading us from the visible to the invisible. We learn to believe in and see the heights and depths of reality. It is no surprise, then, that living a true and sincere sacramental life will gradually open up this reality not just within the liturgical and communal life of the Church, but also in our personal, devotional life.

Likewise, a church with no Mysteries, or even an Orthodox community with a lack of formation in the Mysteries, will eventually lose the sense of this supernatural reality. The danger, again, is that such a community becomes centered on this world, diminishing its joy in the present experience of heavenly life and losing its longing for eternal life.

PSALM 15 (16)

"He has manifested His wonders to His saints"

A school teacher from Luxor was suffering from acute migraine headaches that attacked him daily for several hours. The pain was so intense that he could not prevent himself from weeping. A doctor prescribed certain medications, but he decided he would visit St. Pope Kyrillos VI before taking them.

After waiting at the Patriarchate for the other visitors to leave, he turned to the Saint and asked, "Do I also get a blessing?" The Pope motioned for him to kneel and placed his hand Cross exactly on the location of the pain.

The man immediately felt an intense heat and he sensed the pain from the headache diminishing with a sudden feeling of peace. He then said to His Holiness, "Pray for me because I suffer from painful headaches." The Saint tenderly patted him on the shoulder saying, "That is what I am doing, my son!" He thanked him and left. Later that day he waited to see if the headache would return, but nothing happened and they never returned.

On How Gratitude Provokes God

St. Isaac the Syrian says that gratitude on the part of the receiver provokes the giver to bestow even greater gifts. What a beautiful spiritual law for us to always keep before us! Simeon the Elder waited his whole life to see Christ, and in his gratitude for just a few moments of holding the Child Jesus in his arms, exclaimed, "Lord, now you are letting Your servant depart in peace for my eyes have seen Your salvation..." (Lk 2:29). In reality, we have been granted much greater gifts than Simeon if we only reflect on our Baptism, the indwelling of the Holy Spirit, the gift of the Eucharist, the mystery of Confession, and many other precious jewels.

If we come to understand that everything we are and everything we have–both what appears to be good and even what seems to be lacking–as a perfect gift coming from the hands of a good and loving Father, then gratitude will spring up in the depths of our hearts, provoking God to grant us even more. St. John Chrysostom likens the soul that gives thanks in times of evil circumstances to the same dignity of the martyrs. Gratitude is an indication that one is looking with singleness of devotion toward God. One cannot be grateful if he is envious or jealous of others.

Likewise, growing in gratitude requires that we pay attention to the seemingly small and inconsequential matters that pass by us at every moment. Have we ever rejoiced in gratitude to God for an egg? I'll never forget what a pious lady that I was blessed to know shared with me about St. Pope Kyrillos and eggs! Once when she was visiting him in Cairo, he requested that breakfast be brought to them which included some hard boiled eggs. He proceeded to take one of the eggs and very carefully and meticulously peel it, all the while admiring its beauty. He then held the egg up, turning it from one angle to the next, and said to the lady, "Do you see how much God loves us?!"

PSALM 18 (19)

"From my secret sins, cleanse me O Lord"

St. Pope Kyrillos VI, like so many other saints, had the spiritual discernment to know when to deal with a soul gently or when it was necessary at times to deal with the soul harshly.

A young man for a long time had been far from the church. One day he had the desire to see St. Pope Kyrillos VI, but the Pope's secretary wouldn't let him in, saying that His Holiness was resting. The young man lied and said, "Look, I am not a Christian and I have a reason to see your Pope; why are you trying to prevent me from seeing him?" The secretary, deceived by the trick, started thinking it was probably inappropriate to prevent a guest of the church from seeing the Pope.

As they were talking, the Saint came out of his cell, looked at the young man with a piercing intensity and in a loud voice reproved him saying, "Do you renounce your Christ in order to see a Patriarch? Get out of here! Get out!"

The man left feeling humiliated. He wandered about in the gardens of the Patriarchate not knowing what to do. He sat down and began weeping. His conscience hounded him for days and he felt he had no choice but to go back to the Pope and ask for his forgiveness and absolution. When he returned, he was surprised to find a big, kind, and compassionate heart. The Saint gave him his blessing and helped the young man straighten out his life by placing him on the path of repentance.

On Spiritual Mourning

There are no limits to man's repentance in this life. As one's heart is enlarged, becoming more like Christ's own heart, repentance is offered not only for oneself but for the whole creation, including those whose hearts are hardened and opposed to God. St. Paul wrote to the Philippians, "As I have told you before, and now remind you with tears, many live as enemies of the Cross of Christ. Their end is destruction. Their god is their stomach. Their glory is their shame. Their minds are set on earthly things" (Php 3:18, 19).

"Blessed are those who mourn, for they shall be comforted" (Mt 5:4). There is a vast difference between spiritual mourning and earthly mourning, and between natural tears and spiritual tears. Natural sadness or mourning comes from earthly needs that are unmet. This is usually accompanied by despair, which is a lack of hope. Spiritual mourning and tears come from our desire to be close to God, not to offend God, the desire to be perfect, and our longing for heaven and God alone. But, because of sin, our love moves us to weep. These tears, though, are mixed with joy and hope because God consoles us. "Those who sow in tears shall reap in joy" (Ps 125:5). St. John Climacus calls it "joyful sadness."

One of the saints was confessing his sins to a younger priest while sobbing throughout. The confessor was surprised as he saw no correlation between the sins that he had confessed and his disconsolate weeping. When he remarked to the saint about this, the Elder replied, "Son, you think sin is the breaking of a law? No, son, sin is the betrayal of love. What has the Lord done for me and what have I done for Him?" He was convinced that he had not adequately responded to God's goodness to him. If we grow in both the self-knowledge of our sins and weaknesses, as well as the goodness and love of God, we would say with one of the Desert Fathers, "If I were allowed to see my sins, three or four men would not be enough to weep for them."

PSALM 24 (25)

"My eyes are ever looking toward the Lord, for He alone will draw my feet out of the snare"

St. Pope Kyrillos VI faced much opposition throughout his service as Patriarch. Particularly painful were wounds inflicted from within the Church. Satan planted hate and envy toward the Saint in the hearts of twelve important Cairo-based priests. The priests organized themselves and printed pamphlets defaming the Pope. They would often be up until 1:30 a.m. each day preparing these pamphlets and distributing them to various churches. This went on for a year and a half!

One day, the printer did not function. When they tried to fix it and restart the printing, it would break again. They started fearing that God was not supporting their action. The senior priest of the group went to visit the Pope:

"I have sinned, absolve me, Your Holiness."

The Saint asked, "What is the matter, my son?"

The priest responded, "I insulted you very much, Your Holiness!"

The Pope responded, "Staying up till 1:30 in the morning every day, printing pamphlets and distributing them from Alexandria to Aswan, until the printer broke..." Astonished, the priest then said, "You know all of this, Your Holiness?!"

The Pope began listing the names of all the priests participating, leaving the priest astonished at how much he knew. The priest asked, "Why didn't you talk to us?" The Saint lamented, "I was praying for you."

The priest said, "I have sinned, please absolve me Your Holiness." The Pope answered, "With all my heart, I absolve you, my son." Then the priest asked, "Should I bring my colleagues, Your Holiness?" The Pope answered, "Why not, my son? Let them come." The priest asked, "Will you absolve them, Your Holiness?" The Saint answered, "With all my heart, I absolve them, my son."

The group of priests all came to visit the Pope and receive his blessing. They remained his most faithful servants up until his departure from this world.

On the Silence of a Wounded Heart

After His Resurrection, Jesus did not castigate the disciples for having abandoned Him. He did not even utter a word to St. Peter about denying Him three times. Many of us would not resist the opportunity of pointing out to others how they disappointed or hurt us. But Jesus displays the utmost kindness and gentleness: "Peace be with you" (Jn 20:19, 21).

The whole of the life of Christ is characterized by restraint. There is no one else in human history who had a right to speak more than Jesus. And yet, the first thirty years of His life are wrapped in silence. We find that same silent disposition in both the Mother of God and St. Joseph. There is an important spiritual principle here for all of us. Before being people of action and outward service, we should give priority to the interior and secret life between the soul and God. We must be like the pure Mother of God who "kept all these things and pondered them in her heart" (Lk 2:19).

The silence of Jesus' wounded heart reaches its climax in His Passion. "Like a sheep led to the slaughter, He opened not His mouth" (Is 53:7). They said of Jesus, "No man ever spoke like this Man!" (Jn 7:46). But it could equally be said, "No man ever knew how to keep silent like this Man!" Interior grief and sorrow are like precious perfumes by which we join and share in Christ's suffering. But if we, instead, seek human consolation by always divulging them to others, then just like the fragrance, they dissipate.

Like with every virtue, we need discernment in its application. There are times when we will need to unburden our hearts to others and there should be no shame in this. "There is a time to keep silence and a time to speak" (Ec 3:7).

PSALM 26 (27)

"My heart says of You, seek His face...do not hide Your face from me"

A Christian man was speaking with his non-Christian colleague at the university. The non-Christian colleague said to him, "I like your Pope and I experience a deep peace when I am in his presence. That's why I am going now to meet him again. Would you like to come with me?"

Surprised by this, the Christian man answered him, "Did you make an appointment for this visit?" He replied, "You don't need an appointment to see the Pope. His door is open for everyone."

They decided to go together. The Christian colleague had neither seen nor met St. Pope Kyrillos VI before and knew nothing about him. Entering was easy and no appointment was necessary. During their visit, the Saint turned to them and said, "I am always like this. My door is open for everyone, at any time without an appointment." They were astonished; it was as though the Pope was listening to them and then repeating their conversation!

On Living in Wonder

Our God is a God of wonder: "Who is like You, O Lord, among the gods? Who is like You, glorious in holiness, fearful in praises, doing wonders?" (Ex 15:11). God's wonder means that He is perfect in creativity, surprise, and beauty. When Jesus told them to take away the stone from the tomb of Lazarus who had been dead already for four days, Martha objected: "Lord, by this time there is a stench, for he has been dead four days" (Jn 11:39). Jesus said to her, "Did I not say to you that if you would believe you would see the glory of God?" (Jn 11:40). Jesus encourages us to maintain a sense of wonder in our relationship with God.

Children naturally live in wonder. Their world is always full of surprises, things to marvel at and admire. Unfortunately, as we lose that natural simplicity with age, we also lose our ability to live in wonder. But in holiness we recover that sense of wonder, growing in greater admiration, newness, and appreciation for the things of God. We can cultivate the sense of wonder by learning to meditate, ponder, and reflect more deeply on the Scriptures, the lives of the saints, and on nature. When one of the saints held a beautiful flower in her hand, inflamed by its beauty and with love for God, she said, "And God, then, has thought from all eternity of creating this flower for love of me!"

It is clear that the Church has received from Christ the importance of meditating on His Passion. Nearly one-third of the Synoptic Gospels and one half of St. John's are dedicated to the last week of Jesus' life. The Holy Week service–just in terms of the magnitude of hours spent in Church, the number of readings from both the Old and New Testaments–all indicate the need to remain in wonder at our Lord's sacrifice. The Eucharist is also a Mystery (Sacrament) of wonder. Our preparation for the Eucharist is not just about our sins and asking for forgiveness, but growing more in the understanding of the love of Jesus revealed in the Eucharist toward us. Living in wonder prepares us to be ready for the wonders of God. "Look among the nations, and see; wonder and be astounded. For I will work a work in your days which you would not believe, though it were told you" (Hab 1:5).

PSALM 62 (63)

"My soul clings tightly to You, Your right hand has upheld me"

In 1961, an abbot and bishop of a monastery in Egypt was disseminating offensive letters against St. Pope Kyrillos VI. The Holy Synod of the Church met to investigate and discuss the matter, as well as some accusations against the same abbot. The Pope said to the members of the Synod, "I am so sad at the beginning of my patriarchate, to stand in a trial of a bishop; in any event, do not mention any accusations against this bishop that are related to me. I forgive him and am rescinding my rights."

On another occasion in 1968, one of Cairo's most influential newspapers whose editor-in-chief was a prominent politician published a front page editorial attacking St. Pope Kyrillos' financial transactions.

The Pope had just concluded some meetings and was on his way to his private residence. One of his spiritual children asked him, "Your Holiness, what is this written in the newspaper?" The Pope responded, "The editor-in-chief called me a while ago and agreed to publish my reply to his attack."

The man said to the Pope, "Don't reply! In your silence the Lord shall defend you. We all defend you with our lives." The look in the Pope's eyes was deeply touching as he repeated the words, "The LORD will fight for you, and you shall hold your peace" (Ex 14:14). The Pope never defended himself in the newspaper.

On Forgiving Others

If we take seriously our divine filiation as Christians, then we come to realize just as equally our divine fraternity with one another. St. John Kolobos (the Short) said that the spiritual life is built on the foundation of our neighbor. Jesus devotes a significant portion of His teachings to the love of neighbor. There is no escaping that my life is tied to my neighbor. "And forgive us our trespasses, as we forgive them that trespass against us" (Mt 6:12).

It is not simply a matter of a commandment; forgiveness of others goes to the heart of our attitude toward God Himself. We can only venerate and respect every soul, no matter how wayward, when we come to understand how much God loves that soul. We can easily imagine how we, earthly parents, would react to someone trying to impress us with how much they say they love us while at the same time despising or harming our son or daughter. The late saintly Fr. Bishoy Kamel in a prayer said, "They are your children, O Lord. Some are good, others are evil, others are wasting themselves... they all have one thing in common: they are Your children. I am the servant of Your children and have no right to insult or despise any of them, because if I do, I would be insulting You or despising You."

St. Paul wrote, "And be kind to one another, tenderhearted, forgiving one another, even as God in Christ forgave you" (Eph 4:32). The source of forgiveness is a merciful heart. God forgives us because He is Merciful Love. Lack of forgiveness is always a symptom of a hardened heart. But, lack of forgiveness is also a sign of a lack of faith. Refusing to forgive is a way of clinging to my rights and getting my due now because I really do not believe that God can do better for me. If I truly trust that God can and will bring good out of every situation, then I am free to let go and forgive with a peaceful heart.

PSALM 66 (67)

"Let the peoples praise You O God, let all the peoples praise You"

In 1969, a certain deacon was assigned to pray the Divine Liturgy serving inside the Sanctuary with St. Pope Kyrillos VI on Sundays, Wednesdays and Fridays each week. After midnight on a Tuesday morning, St. Pope Kyrillos appeared to him in a vision as he was fast asleep. The Pope was holding the Cross in his right hand and woke him up from his sleep saying, "Arise, my son, I need you." Knowing that Tuesday was not his turn to serve liturgy with the Pope, he went back to sleep only for the saintly Pope to appear in another vision and awaken him again saying, "Arise, my son, I need you." He went back to sleep yet again for the second time, only for the Pope to appear to him a third time. In an unusually harsh tone he spoke to him saying, "You don't want to come?! Do you want me to bring the *Prosphora* (offertory bread) and celebrate the Divine Liturgy here, in your home?"

After the third vision, the deacon arose, dressed, and went to the Cathedral. It was dark as it was before 5:00 a.m. St. Pope Kyrillos walked in with his usual reverence, which filled the Cathedral with a very profound, spiritual sense. Having reached the Altar, he knelt before it. Then, the other clergy and people who were present greeted him by making a prostration (*metanoia*) before him. When the deacon tried to do the same, the Pope refused his greetings until he finished the morning prayers.

The deacon then went to him and apologized for what happened, promising never to do that again. The Saint then smiled at him with great fatherly love and answered him, "The next time you will listen and obey, my son." To this he responded, "Yes, I will, *Sayedna* [Master]." The Pope then prayed and blessed his vestments and he prayed the Divine Liturgy with him.

On Being Led by the Holy Spirit

The Gospel tells us that immediately after His baptism in the Jordan River, "Jesus was led up by the Spirit into the wilderness..." (Mt 4:1). The pattern of Jesus' life is both a recapitulation of the experience of the Israelites in the Old Testament, as well as the model, or pattern, of our own journey in the spiritual life. The Israelites who were enslaved in Egypt, were led by God through the wilderness to eventually enter the Promised Land. Jesus, likewise, would go to Egypt as a child, be led by the Holy Spirit into the wilderness, and eventually enter Jerusalem where, on the Cross, He inaugurated the Kingdom of God, the true Promised Land. You and I, too, must be freed from enslavement in Egypt (sin and death) through Holy Baptism, where we receive the Holy Spirit, Who will lead us through the sojourn of the desert of our lives until we are received into the Heavenly Jerusalem.

The number forty in the Scriptures usually denotes a time of trial, preparation, or completion. The forty years of the Israelites and the forty days of Jesus' temptations in the wilderness remind us that our whole earthly life is a time of preparation, trial, and completion. The desert, or the wilderness, is the place of trial, preparation, struggle, and longing. But it is also the place of trust, divine companionship, joyful expectation, and love. It is the Spirit of God (the gift of God Himself) dwelling in us (Ro 8:11), Who is our Guide, Companion, Director, and Comforter. "For as many as are led by the Spirit of God, these are sons of God" (Ro 8:14). But we are never alone; we are not guided by a Law (Ga 5:18), but by the Divine Lawgiver Himself. God is not waiting for us at the finish line, but our Friend and Shepherd carries us on His shoulders. And all along the way, He whispers to us tenderly, "Do not fear, little flock, for it is your Father's good pleasure to give you the kingdom" (Lk 12:32).

PSALM 69 (70)

"As for me, I am poor and needy; hasten to my aid O God"

A certain man was a factory manager in Alexandria from 1955 until its nationalization in 1963. When the newly delegated supervisor came after the takeover, the original factory manager was referred to public prosecution on false accusations. A partial investigation was carried out by the intelligence department. The factory manger lived in fear for about five months between inquiries and being released on bail; his life was a nightmare.

One day, he went to St. Mark's Cathedral in Alexandria where St. Pope Kyrillos VI was leading Vespers. During the time when the Pope was censing the Altar, the man went to the Sanctuary and knelt in front of the Saint and kissed his hand. He intended to tell him about his problem and ask for his prayers for him and his family, but he was greatly amazed when he heard the Pope saying, "Why are you afraid? Do not be worried! God is with you. St. Mina is going to be by your side. Maintain your strength." The Saint then prayed for him and the man did not say a word of what he intended to tell him. He realized that he knew everything already.

In less than a month, the clouds dispersed as he was proven innocent and restored to his position.

On Fear During Trials

One of Satan's greatest tactics in spiritual warfare is diversion. To be diverted is to be turned away from what is most important or from one's goal. And what is most important and our ultimate goal is our relationship with God and our preparation for eternal life. In the Divine Liturgy, the priest, with arms outstretched, cries out on behalf of all and says, "Lead us throughout the way into Your Kingdom!" Satan wants nothing more than to divert us in order to make sure this prayer is not realized.

It is not difficult for each of us to acknowledge the many ways we are diverted every day from what is most important, spending our time and energy on the lesser things and delaying for another time the greater things of our salvation. But one major, proven tool in Satan's arsenal is fear. He wants us to be afraid of everything except, of course, from the only things we should fear—despising God through sin and carelessness, and neglecting our judgment on the last day. Jesus says, "Do not be afraid of those who kill the body but cannot kill the soul. Rather, be afraid of the One Who can destroy both soul and body in hell" (Mt 10:28). Fear is based on love for something, and a desire not to lose it. We do not fear the loss of something we do not love or value. In this sense, it is completely understandable and natural to fear the loss of many good, temporal things. However, what gives us the strength to overcome or endure our fear is valuing something else more of greater value than that which we risk losing.

Fear blinds us, or rather makes us nearsighted, by shifting our focus on one thing to the exclusion of everything else. When fear tempts you to divert your attention away from God, say with St. Paul, "I press on toward the finishing line to win the heavenly prize to which God has called me in Christ Jesus" (Php 3:14).

PSALM 112 (113)

"He raises the poor from the dust and lifts the needy from the rubbish heap"

When St. Pope Kyrillos VI was visiting Kafr El Sheikh in the Nile Delta of Lower Egypt, hundreds of people exuberantly gathered around him. At one point the Saint spontaneously turned to a man among the crowd and said, "It seems that you sell falafel!" The man was amazed and answered, "Yes, Your Holiness, this is true." So the Pope said to him, "I would like to eat some of your falafel."

The man went out full of excitement that the Pope wanted to eat from his food. But some people close by whispered to His Holiness that this might disappoint those who prepared a big feast with more expensive food for his visit. But he said to them, "Let him go, I want to please him and make him happy!"

On God's Joy

Jesus, the Word Incarnate, is the Image of the invisible God (Col 1:15). In coming into the world, Christ affirms throughout His teaching ministry, His Death, and His Resurrection that in seeing Him we have seen God (Jn 14:9). The Face of Jesus, St. Paul tells us (2 Co 4:6), is the glory of God. In Christ we find the heart of God Who is merciful, peaceful, compassionate, sensitively aware, generous, humble, and joyful.

We might not normally think of joy as an attribute of God. But actually we find in Jesus the joy that we bring to God. "In that hour Jesus rejoiced in the Spirit and said, 'I thank You, Father, Lord of heaven and earth, that You have hidden these things from the wise and prudent and revealed them to babes. Even so, Father, for so it seemed good in Your sight'" (Lk 10:21).

Joy is inseparably linked to love. If God loves us unconditionally, then it is also true that we are a cause of His joy. But Jesus does not simply want to relay to us the joy of God, He wants to give it to us. "These things I have spoken to you, that My joy may be in you, and that your joy may be made full" (Jn 15:11).

The first of God's joys toward us is our creation in His Image and Likeness which He declared to be "very good" (Ge 1:31). The second joy is that of our adoption, our divine filiation. Being in Christ, we likewise hear the words in our hearts, "This is My beloved Son in Whom I am well pleased!" (Mt 3:17). The third joy is that of our elevation to friendship with God: "No longer do I call you servants, for a servant does not know what his master is doing; but I have called you friends, for all things that I heard from My Father I have made known to you" (Jn 15:15). The fourth of God's joys is that He is our Savior, an endless ocean of mercy and forgiveness: "I say to you that likewise there will be more joy in heaven over one sinner who repents than over ninety-nine just persons who need no repentance" (Lk 15:7). And the fifth joy is that of our eternal glory with Him: "It is your Father's good pleasure to give you the kingdom" (Lk 12:32). "Enter into the joy of your Lord" (Mt 25:13).

PSALM 142 (143)

"Teach me to do Your will, for You are my God"

After she graduated from college, a young woman felt a strong yearning toward monasticism. She wanted to become a bride to the heavenly Bridegroom. But she was not certain if this was truly her calling or a passing phase in her life.

One day after receiving Holy Communion at the hands of St. Pope Kyrillos VI, she stood silently entreating the Lord and asking for His will. At that moment she heard St. Pope Kyrillos calling out for her from a distance and saying to her, "He tells you this is His will!"

Surprised and stunned, she asked, "Who is 'He,' Your Holiness?" The Pope replied, "Aren't you asking God what His will is? He says to you this is His will." Without any hesitation, she forsook the world and followed God's will.

On Discernment and Spiritual Perception

When they asked St. Antony the Great which of the virtues was the greatest, he replied, "Discernment," which he called the "lantern of the soul." Discernment includes wisdom, the ability of "seeing the whole picture" and understanding the why and purpose behind all things. It also refers to the grace to know the Will of God. As a charismatic gift of the Church, discernment is also a unique manifestation in the lives of the saints given by God to lead other souls to salvation. Likewise, St. John Climacus in the *Ladder of Divine Ascent* describes the progression of discernment. First, beginners start with self-knowledge. At a middle level, one can distinguish between what is truly good and what is opposed to the good. Finally, the perfection of discernment is attained with knowledge resulting from divine illumination.

Regarding discernment as enlightened spiritual perception, Jesus said, "The lamp of the body is the eye. Therefore, when your eye is good, your whole body also is full of light. But when your eye is bad, your body also is full of darkness" (Lk 11:34). The word "good" is perhaps better translated as "sound" or "single" (Greek *aplous*) and refers to singleness of devotion, or attention. It is another way of saying "purity of heart." Pure honey is honey that is not mixed with anything else. In the same way, the heart is pure when its attention is single and soundly devoted to God.

The opposite of single vision is double vision, a divided heart, or what St. James calls a "double-minded (literally a "two-souled") man unstable in all his ways" (Jas 1:8). The perfect Man, Jesus Christ, is the exemplar of the "pure in heart," because He was unified and perfect in His love and obedience to the Father. He never wavered, was never distracted, and never desired independence from the Father's Will. "For I have come down from heaven, not to do My own will, but the will of Him who sent Me" (Jn 6:38).

The Third Hour

PSALM 19 (20)

"Hear us in the day we call upon You"

In 1966, a man was afflicted with an ear disease that almost left him deaf. He sought medical help for two years and had his tonsils taken out, but all to no avail. He was then told that he needed an expensive surgery on both of his ears, which he could not afford. Saddened, he resigned himself to the reality that his ears would never be cured.

In September 1969, he went to Cairo again seeking medical help. There, another doctor confirmed the previous diagnosis. On a Tuesday in September 1969, he headed to the Cathedral in Cairo where St. Pope Kyrillos VI was. He found the Pope praying, so he went up to him, and amazingly about three meters before he reached him, the Saint said to him, "Are your ears bothering you? Have faith that God will heal you."

The man bowed down and kissed the Saint's hand. The Pope put his hands on his ears and prayed for a long time, and afterward he asked his personal deacon to give the man a piece of cotton anointed with holy oil. The Saint said to him, "Son, when you go to sleep, split the piece of cotton into two pieces and put half into each ear. God willing you will have no need for surgery."

The man left very happy. Before going to sleep that night he did what the Saint told him to do. Typically, he was not able to sleep for more than two hours because of the pain but when he put the pieces of cotton in his ears it was like an anesthetic. He slept for nine hours and when he awoke, his ears were cured.

On the Impetus in Personal Prayer

There are many reasons why we pray and many ways to pray. But what should be the compelling force that stirs us to prayer every day? What reason for prayer can withstand our shifting emotions and needs? Early in the Gospel according to St. Mark we read that Jesus "went up on the mountain and called to Him those He Himself wanted. And they came to Him...that they might be with Him..." (Mk 3:13-14). The simple and most profound reason for each of us to set aside time every day for prayer is because Jesus wants and calls us just to be with Him. If we can begin any conversation about prayer with this image always before us, a huge weight will be lifted off of our shoulders in terms of the quality or success of our prayer life.

We often think that prayer is something we do, but if we shift our understanding to the truth that prayer is more about what God wants to do in us, we will be less likely to worry so much about the quality of our prayer. If we give time every day to personal prayer, we can be sure that God is successful regardless of how poor and miserable our own efforts are. As one nun toward the end of a long life remarked, "I never have the satisfaction of feeling that I prayed."

When Jesus called His disciples to be with Him, it was not to interview them or scrutinize them, but to love them and reveal Himself to them. The same principle applies to us. The essential fruit of prayer is to know God as "Abba, Father." To know God as Father means also accepting that our deepest identity is that we are His children and recipients of His unconditional and gratuitous love. Every other fruit of prayer, including the boldness of approaching Him with our petitions, must grow out of this experience.

PSALM 22 (23)

"Your mercy shall follow me all the days of my life"

A man had heart disease and whenever he felt chest pain he would go to St. Pope Kyrillos and as soon as he would give him his blessing, the pain would disappear. In the last days of the Saint's life, the Pope himself was very sick and the doctors forbade anyone to meet him, no matter the importance of the visitor or the urgency of the matter.

The man wanted to just catch a glimpse of the Saint, even from a distance. So, he went to the Patriarchate and waited outside his door. By chance, his secretary opened his door and His Holiness saw him. He got up from his bed while he was very sick and came toward him in an extremely warm, welcoming way. The man yelled in shock and pleaded with the Pope not to move but the Pope kept on walking toward him, embraced the man and said, "Where have you been, my son? I have missed you very much!" He replied, "I came only to look at you from a distance, my chest is causing me a lot of pain."

"May God save your heart," he said, and started to rub his chest while the man kept entreating the Pope not to exert himself. But the Saint did not heed his plea and kept praying for a long time until the pain was gone. He then blessed him and walked him to the door. That was the last time he saw him; later that week the Lord called the Saint home to heaven.

On Self-Forgetfulness

One of the saints said that to love is not difficult; we begin to love as soon as we cease to think of ourselves. One means of describing the journey of the spiritual life is the lifelong movement along a spectrum from inordinate self-love to selfless love, or self-forgetfulness. The Fathers tell us that self-love is linked to our pride and to our attachment to carnal and sensual pleasure. It leads us to be overly sensitive and self-absorbed, leaving us unavailable to love our neighbor in a Christ-like way.

It is in the Gospel where we encounter not only the words and acts of Jesus, but His attitudes and interior dispositions. When we meditate on His life, we will love Him more, and through this love we will derive the strength, along with God's grace, to imitate Him. "Let each of you look not only to his own interests, but also to the interests of others. Have this mind among yourselves, which is yours in Christ Jesus, Who, though He was in the form of God, did not count equality with God a thing to be grasped, but emptied Himself, taking the form of a servant..." (Php 2:4-7). St. Paul is telling us to have this as an active and dynamic disposition in our life, not simply a reactionary one. We will then desire to say, to both God and my neighbor, with St. John the Baptist, "He must increase, but I must decrease" (Jn 3:30).

When God takes possession of my thoughts and my will, I will come to see that, apart from God, I am "nothingness." My very existence depends and belongs to Him. All my disturbances come from thinking of myself to be something of importance and claiming rights to myself that in reality I do not possess. "He who finds his life will lose it, and he who loses his life for My sake will find it" (Mt 10:39).

PSALM 23 (24)

"The Lord of Hosts, He is the King of Glory"

In 1969, St. Pope Kyrillos VI called one of the bishops at midnight to come and pray with him while he was at the dependency of St. Antony's monastery in Cairo. So, upon the Saint's request, the Pope's driver took them by car to the church of St. Barbara in Old Cairo.

When they arrived, they found the large wooden gate closed. The driver tried to open the gate but could not. Then, the personal disciple of His Holiness tried to open it but he also could not. The bishop himself subsequently tried to open it but he, likewise, was unsuccessful. Finally, the Saint approached the gate and made the sign of the Cross on it and said, "Lift up your heads, O you gates! And be lifted up, you everlasting doors! And the King of glory shall come in" (Ps 23:7).

Instantly, the gates opened by themselves, and those who were standing by watching, were left in amazement.

On the Gifts of the Holy Spirit

In describing the work of the Holy Spirit in the Church and in the life of the believer, we can delineate between two kinds of gifts of the Holy Spirit: *charismatic* and *sanctifying*. *Charismatic* gifts of the Holy Spirit are more outward forms of the manifestation of the Spirit and typically related to the ministry of the Church. They include the gifts of miracles, healings, speaking in tongues, prophesying, visions, and discernment of spirits.

These gifts are given for the edification, or building up, of the Church and aid in the spread of the Gospel and the strengthening of the people of God. Though such gifts are usually entrusted to humble and holy people, they are not, in and of themselves, evidence or rewards for personal holiness. In fact, our Lord warned us, "Many will say to Me in that day, 'Lord, Lord, have we not prophesied in Your name, cast out demons in Your name, and done many wonders in Your name?' And then I will declare to them, 'I never knew you; depart from Me, you who practice lawlessness!'" (Mt 7:22-23).

Then, there are *sanctifying* gifts of the Holy Spirit that are given to all Christians to make us into the image of Christ. It is these gifts that make us saints, not the *charismatic* gifts, for they are the characteristics of the Spirit of Christ. St. Ambrose of Milan (On the Mysteries, 7:42) and other early Fathers understood that these seven gifts are given to us in Baptism and Chrismation. They were prophesied in Isaiah: "There shall come forth a rod from the root of Jesse and a flower shall grow out of his root. The Spirit of God shall rest upon Him, the Spirit of Wisdom and Understanding, the Spirit of Counsel and Might, the Spirit of Knowledge and Godliness. The Spirit of the fear of God shall fill Him" (Is 11:1-3).

The gifts remind us of the interiority of the Gospel and the Spirit of Christ. They work in two primary ways toward God and spiritual perfection. First, by the enlightenment of the intellectual faculty through which we perceive truth. And second, by the strengthening of the will which moves us either toward or away from what the intellect perceives is good or evil. The gifts help us to respond to the presence of the Holy Spirit and we cultivate them through our life of purity, repentance, prayer, and other ascetical works.

PSALM 25 (26)

"I have placed my trust in the Lord...Your mercy is before my eyes"

In 1968, a certain man had an emergency appendectomy as his appendix was about to perforate. But God saved his life. After the operation, he was in severe agony asking for any sedative medication to ease the intensity of his pain. He prayed to God asking for the intercession of St. Pope Kyrillos VI, then slept and dreamt that the Saint was blessing him.

After he recovered and left the hospital, he went to see the Pope and said to him, "I saw Your Holiness in my dream." St. Pope Kyrillos immediately replied, "You are the man who had an appendectomy," and he tapped him with his hand Cross over the place of the surgical incision. The man left perplexed saying, "I don't know how the Pope knew that I was 'the man who had an appendectomy' and how he visited me at night in my dream."

On the Gifts of Wisdom and Understanding

The gift of Wisdom reveals to us how the goodness of God underlies everything. It grants us the ability to see the whole, and how everything fits together. It is likened to the perspective of an architect who sees a complete picture, as opposed to a subcontractor who only sees a part. Or like the conductor of a symphony who hears each and every instrument, as opposed to a performer of one instrument. We begin to look at the world as God sees it, with His perspective, and how everything fits together. It means understanding the "why" and the "purpose" of things which lead us to love God more. "But he who is joined to the Lord is one spirit with Him" (1 Co 6:17).

The gift of Understanding helps us penetrate divine mysteries, the Holy Scriptures and sacred texts, teachings, and doctrines of the Church. It gives us the inner meaning of divine truth. St. Paul wrote:

> 'Eye has not seen, nor ear heard, nor have entered into the heart of man the things which God has prepared for those who love Him.' But God has revealed them to us through His Spirit. For the Spirit searches all things, yes, the deep things of God. For what man knows the things of a man except the spirit of the man which is in him? Even so no one knows the things of God except the

> Spirit of God. Now we have received, not the spirit of the world, but the Spirit who is from God, that we might know the things that have been freely given to us by God (1 Co 2:9-12).

It is love that activates the gifts of the Holy Spirit, which in turn grants us this penetration into the divine, further inflaming love within the soul.

PSALM 28 (29)

"The Lord will give strength to His people. The Lord will bless His people with peace"

In May 1970, a woman received an accidental blow to her right eye while on the bus going to her final exams in law school. She did not pay much attention to it, especially since it did not show any injuries at the time. After some time, she developed a severe headache and intense eye pain. However, she decided to have it examined at a future time.

Four months later, in September, she went to Cairo to receive her law degree. She decided to stop by the Cathedral to give thanks to the Lord for the success of her exams. At the Cathedral's main entrance, she found a large crowd as it was both the Feast of the Cross and the ordination of a new bishop. Finding it difficult to go in, she went around the Papal residence to the back door and there she saw St. Pope Kyrillos VI.

She approached him and tried to kiss the Cross in his hand as was customary, but the Pope pulled it away, hit her hand with the Cross and lifted the Cross up. She tried again to reach out and hold the Cross to kiss it, and again he hit her hand with it and then placed the Cross on her painful eye and began to pray. He then left to his cell on the top floor. She stood there astonished and unable to move. She said to a lady who was nearby watching, "How did His Holiness know that my right eye was sore? I was on my way to have it tested!"

Receiving no answer, she went to the main door of the Patriarchate and saw a priest standing at the entrance of the ground floor of the Papal residence preventing people from going upstairs. She told him what happened and asked, "How could His Holiness know about the pain in my right eye, although there is no visible mark or sign to show it is sore?!" The Reverend Father answered, "My daughter, the Pope is an angel on earth." She replied, "Truly, we have lived to see an angel and saint among us!"

On the Gifts of Counsel and Fortitude (Might)

"But the Helper, the Holy Spirit, whom the Father will send in My name, he will teach you all things, and bring to your remembrance all things that I said to you" (Jn 14:26). The Holy Spirit dwells in us to counsel us by both recalling the teachings of Christ and also applying them to actual circumstances. How many times in our life are we left perplexed, seeking to make the right choices pleasing to God? We want to be able to say with Samuel, "Speak, Lord, for your servant is listening!" (1 Sa 3:10).

The gift of Counsel is likened to an antenna, permitting us to pick up the "signal" of God's voice. The gift of Counsel is both practical and mystical, leading us in specific external acts and also in the deep, interior life. The voice of the Holy Spirit is a "still small voice" (1 Ki 19:12), experienced through a dedicated life of prayer and meditation.

The gift of Fortitude comes to strengthen us in our struggles. The demands of divine love are often greater than what is humanly possible without the grace of the Holy Spirit. The life of Christian perfection is not something that can be accomplished through natural, and even, heroic talents. Rather, it is God, Himself, Who accomplishes this work in us. The fortitude of the martyrs is a perfect example of this gift. Which one of us can imagine withstanding the seven years of torture endured by St. George, the Prince of Martyrs?

Our Lord said to the Apostles, "But you shall receive power when the Holy Spirit has come upon you; and you shall be witnesses to Me in Jerusalem, and in all Judea and Samaria, and to the end of the earth" (Ac 1:8). And we are witnesses that these same Apostles, who were afraid to follow Jesus to the Cross, became courageous lions ready to face death for the Name of the Lord.

PSALM 29 (30)

"Oh Lord my God, I cried to You and You healed me"

When St. Pope Kyrillos VI was ordained patriarch, an official group from the region of Damanhour went to congratulate him. When it was one of the group's turn to congratulate the Pope, the Saint asked him, "Are you really from Damanhour?" The man responded that actually he was from Kafer-el Sheik, but he worked in Damanhour.

The Pope smiled and went on to ask him how he was doing. The man sadly replied that his daughter was not doing so well. She was not ill, but she had very grotesque pimples on her skin by the hundreds, and he had spent all he had after bringing her to see many doctors, all to no avail. The only therapy was electric suction of these pimples which was too painful for a child. Furthermore, even after an electric suction there was still no guarantee that the pimples would not return. So, it seemed that treatment was futile.

Upon hearing this, the Saint appeared very distraught and sincerely moved on behalf of the man's daughter. Full of compassion the Pope put his blessed hands on the girl's face, and prayed. Then, he breathed in her face, smiled warmly, and said, "Go! No more pimples!" And, as if what he said was registered in the heavens, three or four days later all the pimples were gone and her face returned as smooth and pure as the face of a baby!

On the Gifts of Knowledge, Piety (Godliness) and Fear

The gift of Knowledge embraces all created things as they are in the hands of the Creator. It encompasses a deeper penetration of the wonders of creation but understands that they are all nothing compared to the reality of God. All human genius and development are seen in the light of God and divine reality. Therefore, the gift of Knowledge shows an appreciation of created things but understands their limitations and priorities. "For what will it profit a man if he gains the whole world, and loses his own soul?" (Mk 8:36). There is a sadder side to the gift of Knowledge–as more is known of the grandeur of creation and the dignity and potential of man, more is also known of the price of evil and sin.

The gift of Piety, or Godliness, is in a sense a "living out" what is known through the gift of Knowledge. It is the gift that brings us to the reverence of God and holy things and shapes our attitudes and behavior based on that reverence. It is the gift of Piety that induces us to revere, kiss, and bow down to the Book of the Gospel because of our knowledge of what this Book is. And it is also the gift of Piety that prompts us to love our enemies, since knowledge instructs us that they are truly God's children.

"Come, you children, hear me: I will teach you the fear of the Lord" (Ps 33:11). With the gift of Fear, the Holy Spirit leads us not so much to fear God and punishment but to fear sin, to fear ourselves and our evil inclinations. St. Paul says, "Therefore, having these promises, beloved, let us cleanse ourselves from all filthiness of the flesh and spirit, perfecting holiness in the fear of God" (2 Co 7:1).

There are two degrees of Fear. The first recognizes the possibility of punishment. This is not the kind of fear that is a gift of the Spirit of Christ. But, it can be a beginning point for hardened sinners. It is not yet love, but it is a form of faith. The second and more perfect way is the fear which is tender love. The fear which would never want to see harm to a relationship–a child with their parent, or a bridegroom for his bride. This is a fear that is the fruit of love.

PSALM 33 (34)

"I sought the Lord, and He answered me; He set me free from all my fears"

On November 25, 1968, a certain young man's father had severe heart disease and was in critical condition. The father asked him to sit down behind him to support his back and to hold the oxygen tube that was assisting his breathing. Minutes later he passed away.

He was still only a young student in the School of Engineering at this time and the image of his father's death haunted him night and day and he was unable to sleep.

One Saturday evening, his mother accompanied him to attend the Vespers service at the new St. Mark's Cathedral in Cairo, but St. Pope Kyrillos VI was not there. They then decided to go to the old Cathedral in Azbakia.

The Saint, who was on his way up to his residence, saw them, turned back and approached them without them having said a word. He put the Cross on the young man's heart and said, "Why are you afraid? Go back home in peace." Immediately, all his fear and anxiety dissipated and a peace enveloped him. They left, glorifying God.

On the Saints and the Spiritual Life

The word "spirituality" does not appear in the Holy Scriptures. What we mean by "spirituality" is simply that Christian life is lived in the power and under the influence of the Holy Spirit. It does not primarily designate this life as dealing with the "spiritual," in the sense of "immaterial." So, if we want to study "spirituality" or "spiritual theology," we have to observe, analyze, absorb, and then, attempt to systematize to some extent, the intersection between the work of the Holy Spirit and an actual human soul. Spirituality is quintessentially "experiential" theology, the study of the saints.

In the New Testament, something radical appears in the understanding of "spirituality." It is no longer simply the experience of a person or nation struggling to know and follow God's law and commandments. But God, Himself, enters human history and the human condition, becomes Man, and demonstrates the meaning and purpose of human existence and fulfillment. He displays human life in the power of the Holy Spirit. Jesus Christ is the portrait of a perfect man, the Saint.

All the saints who "put on" Christ (Ro 13:14) become Christ in another form. Thus it is at once the case that Christ discloses the image of a true saint, while the saint, also, is an incarnation of the beatitudes and an encyclopedia of the work of the Holy Spirit. The saints of every generation are the continued expression of Christ in the world and point us to the authentic path of Christian life. As Thomas Merton so beautifully observed, there are no two saints alike, but they are all like God. Since every human soul is infinitely unique, each one of us is called to be a different, but splendid, image of God; to have our own particular sanctity and yet to be a clear portrait of the Lord Jesus Christ.

PSALM 40 (41)

"But You, O Lord, have mercy on me, and raise me up"

A boy in grade school contracted an undiagnosed disease which made it impossible for him to move his legs. His father had to carry him whenever he needed to move from place to place. They saw several doctors who could not diagnose the problem, but concluded that he probably would not be able to walk again.

His aunt, who had a strong relationship with St. Pope Kyrillos VI, told him about their situation. He gave her a small bottle of holy oil to anoint his legs with and said to her, "Tell them not to be afraid, I will send St. Mina to him this evening at 7:00 p.m. to heal him." The aunt called them and told them what transpired. The family rejoiced and recalled when the Saint healed the father's paralyzed arm on a previous occasion.

The boy's father anointed him with the holy oil and they counted the minutes until 7:00 p.m., the time St. Mina was expected to arrive. They would never forget what happened next. He was lying in bed with his parents around him. The father told him to try and go to sleep but he could not because of the excitement. He was also anxious as to how St. Mina would appear and if it would be frightening seeing such a vision with his eyes. Five minutes before 7:00 p.m. he fell asleep!

When the wall clock struck 7:00 p.m., he was awakened and started jumping in bed. He jumped onto the floor and started running around shouting with excitement, "I can run, Dad! I can run, Mom!" He realized that St. Mina healed him without revealing himself because he knew the boy was afraid.

On the Love of the Saints

"God is love!", St. John exclaims (1 Jn 4:8, 16). Love is not an attribute of God, but directly speaks to His essence. As Trinity, God is a communion of love within Himself. Man was created in this very image of Love, called into being to share in the life of the Holy Trinity. Therefore, the more we draw closer to God, or rather the more He draws closer to us, the more we share in this God-like love, a love that extends to the whole creation. Perfect love was declared to us by our Lord Jesus Christ, Who humbled Himself, became man and suffered and died on our behalf. He enjoined us to share in this redemptive sacrificial love: "Love one another; as I have loved you" (Jn 13:34).

This self-emptying love is a compelling force drawing us to our neighbor, laboring alongside him for his salvation. This is the love that the saints perfected. Have the saints who, while in the flesh, perfected their love for God, lost the capacity to labor for the salvation of others after their departure?

The Church is one and indivisible. "There is neither Jew nor Greek, there is neither slave nor free, there is neither male nor female; for you are all one in Christ Jesus" (Ga 3:28). St. Paul elsewhere says that we are "individually members of one another" (Ro 12:5). Likewise there is no "death" for those in Christ, since in Him death has been destroyed. As we pray in the divine services, "there is no death for your servants but rather a departure." And the Scriptures attest that "God is not the God of the dead, but of the living" (Mt 22:32).

So there is one Church, one Body, made up of those who have departed this world and those of us still struggling in the world. And there can never be a separation between the two; for just as the Body cannot be separated from her Head, so likewise the Body cannot be divided within herself. Indeed if they, while on earth, loved us and prayed fervently for us, how much more now in the presence of Christ will they continue to do the same?

PSALM 42 (43)

"Grant me Your justice, O God, and avenge my case"

One lady was wrongly accused of a crime in a court case and released on bail. She went to St. Pope Kyrillos VI, who comforted her and assured her that God would save her from the trial. The proceedings dragged on. Before each court hearing, she would first go to the Saint who kept telling her, "It will be adjourned." But she kept imploring him saying, "I am tired Your Holiness! Please say I will be proven innocent!" However, he kept repeating to her that the case would be deferred. He even told her details of what the witnesses would testify and what the prosecution would argue.

The case continued for six years. On one occasion, the lady visited the Saint at St. Mina's Monastery in Mariut, and begged him with tears to pray for her. He said to her, "It is over, your innocence has been proven!"

The lady was full of joy and at the next hearing, she was declared innocent. She immediately sent a telegram to the Saint sharing with him the happy news.

On Resentment and Bitterness

The word "resentment" is a compound ("re-sentiment") which means to "feel again." It is typically associated with specific persons or circumstances. We have all struggled with resenting someone for something they said or did to us in the past. Or, perhaps I might be resentful toward God for circumstances in my life that I believe He should have intervened and changed. Bitterness is progressively what I become, what happens to my heart, when anger and resentments are unforgiven and unresolved. It is often described as a change from an experience to a belief or disposition.

Bitterness blocks the grace of God, makes us slaves of inordinate self-love, and destroys fraternal love between us and others. St. Paul warns us, "See to it that no one is deprived of the grace of God, and that no root of bitterness may spring up and cause trouble, resulting in the defilement of many" (Heb 12:15). Elsewhere, St. Paul describes the effect of bitterness as that of "grieving the Holy Spirit of God" (Eph 4:30). Thus, more importantly than their psychological impact, resentment, and bitterness block and frustrate God's work in us and, as St. Paul indicated, make us defiled.

"Now as Jesus passed by, he saw a man who was blind from birth... He spat on the ground and made clay with the saliva; and He anointed the eyes of the blind man with the clay" (Jn 9:1, 6). The blind man never asked Jesus for healing, he had no expectation for receiving back his sight. From his perspective, Jesus' action of spontaneously putting dirt in his eyes and commanding him to stumble his way to the Pool of Siloam before the crowds could have been understood as the height of mockery and embarrassment. Had the blind man been bitter for being blind all these years, he could have easily scoffed or rebuked Christ and missed the greatest miracle of his life, not only receiving his physical sight, but the encounter with the Living God and the salvation of his soul.

PSALM 44 (45)

"I will extol Your Name through all generations"

One day, at the beginning of the establishment of St. Mina's Monastery in Mariut, early in the morning, two fathers went to the Roman well to fill a drum with water. A violent sandstorm struck the area and reduced visibility to less than half a meter. The storm lasted all day until 7:00 p.m. and, thus, the fathers were unable to return to the monastery. All of the monks became extremely worried but there was nothing they could do even though twelve hours had passed.

St. Pope Kyrillos VI was present with them and he was praying in the monastery's small church named after St. Samuel the Confessor. He called for one of the monks and said, "Listen, go straightaway to the fathers and tell them to start the car and come back quickly."

The monk did not argue or complain that it would be impossible with almost zero visibility. Rather, in complete obedience and love, he threw himself in the pitch darkness and started to grope about, not yet realizing that God was leading his every step in response to the prayers of the Saint who sent him. He kept walking a long distance until his knees suddenly hit a metallic object. It was the fathers' car! He praised the Lord Who is marvelous in His Saints! He wondered if he was in the real world or in a world of imagination and illusion!

The sand had completely covered their car. It buried it and filled the inside as well. The fathers and the driver were unconscious. Worried and emotional, the monk, after a few attempts, was able to revive the driver and tell him that the Pope wanted them to return at once to the monastery. As he turned the ignition on, the car started easily. They managed to revive the other fathers, and they gave thanks to God for their safety.

As the monk earlier groped about without any sense of direction, so now did the driver as he drove the car. But how wrong it was to say, "without direction" for after a while the car was about to run right into the church of St. Samuel inside the Monastery. They got out of the car quickly to find the Saint waiting for them with a gentle smile on his face, and the peace which flowed deep from his trusting and faithful heart. In those days, visitors easily lost their way to the monastery in broad daylight, let alone in pitch darkness. It was the Saint's prayers that returned his children safely.

On Reliance and Trust

Throughout the Holy Scriptures, the place of the desert is often associated with purification of the soul, learning reliance upon God and obedience toward Him. The desert is the barren place, stripped of all our necessary support, and leaves us vulnerable. The silence of the desert, devoid of all the noise and distraction of the world, renders it impossible to escape confronting both God and ourselves in honesty and sincerity. The hiddenness and obscurity of the desert are an antidote to our vanity, the constant desire to be noticed and praised for doing great and important things.

Abraham, Moses, Elijah and, of course, the Lord Jesus, were all led into the desert. The desert experience always forces us to make a decision, either to believe and trust in God, or to blaspheme Him. Moses was sanctified in the desert, while others became murderers and thieves. In the desert we either turn to idols or learn to cling to the true God. For the saints of the Old and New Testaments, the desert experience was a release from all earthly support and attachment. There, they realized that all sustenance comes from God and their hope is only in Him.

God wants to strip me of all that is not His, to raise me from mediocrity to true discipleship.

He wants to be the provider of everything in my life, my friend and companion, my food and my light. In the desert, God showered the Israelites with manna, provided them with the column of light and the cloud, and gave them the water from the rock–all of which point to Him, Jesus Christ. There, in the desert, the Lord Himself is my consolation and I come to taste the magnitude of His compassion. I do not need to go out into the physical desert; the desert is within me, my heart is the desert.

PSALM 45 (46)

"Therefore, we will not be afraid, though the earth be shaken"

In 1967, a certain woman who was the principal at a high school in Helwan had just been promoted and understood that there would not be another promotion for a long time.

She went to visit St. Pope Kyrillos VI and saw him sitting by himself with the windows closed talking aloud. She looked around to see who he might be talking to but did not see anyone. He smiled and said, "Who are you looking for?" She questioned him, "Who are you talking to, *Sayedna* ("Master")?" He answered, "Nothing, just..." and did not complete his words. She described the feeling of an electric shock going through her body and in the midst of her confusion he said, "Kafr El Sheik." (Kafr El Sheik is an area in the Nile Delta of Lower Egypt). She responded, "I do not understand." The Saint repeated the same thing, "Kafr El Sheik. Congratulations!" Again, she questioned his words and he just repeated the same thing.

He then prayed for her and said, "God is with you and will raise you above them." She asked, "Above who?" He did not answer but smiled saying, "God will raise you above them; He is with you and will give you strength."

She went home and told her family about the mysterious conversation. The next day she was surprised when her family and friends congratulated her on her promotion to school principal in "Kafr El Sheik" which they read about in that day's newspapers! Her mother went with her to the new city. The school was in the middle of several farms. When they arrived at their new residence, she pulled out her Bible from her luggage and both she and her mother heard a voice saying, "Oof, oof." They looked around but saw nothing.

The next day, when her mother returned home, she slept alone in the house. She woke up seeing shadows of people moving behind the window outside her room. Very frightened, she jumped up and made the sign of the Cross toward the window and the door. She slept in fear each night but forced herself to stay until the end of the week. She recalled the Saint's prayers that God would give her victory over them. At the end of the week she returned home and went to see the Patriarch. Before the

Pope's secretary went in to tell the Pope of her arrival, His Holiness rang on the phone instructing him to let her in.

When the Saint saw her, he kept repeating, "Oof, oof" in the same voice she heard before. Then he said, "They gave you a hard time. I know everything." He gave her some cotton anointed with holy oil and said, "Pray the 'Our Father' and Psalm 90 (91), 'He who dwells in the shelter of the Most High...,' and anoint the windows, doors, and everything in the room. You will have peace from those unblessed ones and I will send St. Mina to you."

When she returned to the house she did the sign of the Cross on everything. It was like a war in the room with voices crying and hurrying to get out! Her body was numb, her hands trembling; she was terrified. Then the voices stopped and she felt comforted and they were gone, forever.

On Temptations

"The kingdom of heaven suffers violence, and the violent take it by force" (Mt 11:12). No Christian is exempt from temptation until Jesus returns in His Second Coming. St. Isaac the Syrian also emphasizes that the nearer we draw to the Kingdom of God, temptations will multiply. The history of humanity, from the Garden of Eden until the end of the world, attests to a great battle between Satan, with his fallen angels, and God. St. Paul is vivid: "For we are not contending against flesh and blood, but against the principalities, against the powers, against the world rulers of this present darkness, against the spiritual hosts of wickedness in the heavenly places" (Eph 6:12).

In this battle, the human soul is the most coveted prize for Satan, because nothing is dearer to God than man. But the victory of Christ over Satan, along with the other two enemies, sin and death, are at the heart of the Christian Gospel. "He disarmed the principalities and powers and made a public example of them, triumphing over them in Him" (Col 2:15). The war has been won, but our work in this world where Satan still has influence and partial reign is to fight the individual battles, by the exercise of our free will, strengthened by the grace of God.

The saints teach us that not only are temptations inevitable, but they are also useful. First, temptations strengthen my will, granting me the opportunity to align my will with God's will. Second, the struggle with temptation ushers in knowledge, of God and myself, and helps me grow in divine wisdom. Third, through temptations, I experience God's grace and consolation. Fourth, temptations elicit the remembrance of God and stir up prayer. Fifth, temptations humble me, preserving me from self-righteousness, fostering me to judge others less. And finally, through temptations, I learn to abandon myself completely to God, "...so that we not put our trust in ourselves but in God who raises the dead" (2 Co 1:9). In all of these, God transforms the times of temptations into crowns of glory in eternity.

PSALM 46 (47)

"Shout to God with cries of gladness. For the Lord, the Most High, is awesome."

The son of a cantor at one of the churches in Alexandria was suffering from dark warts on his face and forehead. His family had a picture of St. Mina the Wonderworker at home that was given to them by St. Pope Kyrillos VI. The son put his face on the picture and said the Lord's Prayer seven times. All the spots disappeared and he recovered.

When the Pope came to Alexandria, the cantor went to receive his blessing. The Saint surprised him by saying, "What did St. Mina do for your son? Do not hide anything!" The man cried with joy and he explained to the Pope exactly what happened. The Saint said, "St. Mina honored you by his visit!"

On Christ our True Rest

"Come to Me, all you who labor and are heavy laden, and I will give you rest. Take My yoke upon you and learn from Me, for I am gentle and lowly in heart, and you will find rest for your souls. For My yoke is easy and My burden is light" (Mt 11:28-30). These are some of the most beautiful and beloved words of the Savior, full of tenderness and compassion, striking deep into the hearts of weary and restless souls. The Greek word for "rest" means much more than relaxation from toil or work, it implies "refreshment" and "nourishment." No man or prophet ever claimed to personally offer such a gift to humanity.

God created man in a state of rest, unity, and harmony with himself, with nature, and with God his Creator. This unity meant that there was no division and peace reigned over all. In Paradise, man did not experience pain, illness, worry or sadness. All this was disturbed after the Fall. When God commanded man to keep the Sabbath, He was reminding man of his original state, granting him a small share in it, and preparing him for the reinstatement of perfect rest in Christ. St. Paul says that the Sabbath was "a shadow of things to come, but the substance is of Christ" (Col 2:17). Christ is our Sabbath, the source of rest, unity, and harmony.

Jesus reveals to us the heart of the Father, Who wants nothing more than to grant us eternal joy. St. John Chrysostom says that Christ calls us not to account for our sins, but to do away with our sins; not because He wants our honor, but because He wants our salvation. Another saint said that, by His incarnation, Jesus came among us as a poor beggar, asking for our love. Hidden behind the words "Give Me a drink" to the Samaritan Woman (Jn 4:7) is Jesus' thirst and desire for us and our salvation. If we seek true happiness and contentment, we will accept Jesus' thirst for our love, and in return offer Him our own love as weak as it may be. Unfortunately, today, as in Jesus' time, many refuse His invitation: "But you are not willing to come to Me that you may have life" (Jn 5:40).

The Sixth Hour

PSALM 53 (54)

"Hear my prayer O God; give ear to the words of my mouth"

After a certain woman's husband died, her father had a house built to provide rental income during the summer season in order to help ease the financial burden of raising the children. Her father handled all the finances including the rent, taxes, and other expenses.

Four years after her husband passed, her father died and she felt overwhelmed not knowing anything about the financial matters. One day, someone from the Department of Taxation came to inform her that she had not paid taxes and they would repossess the house.

She did not know what to do or even where the tax office was. She cried out in prayer, "Oh, Pope Kyrillos! Oh, St. Mina!" Then she decided to take the train to the city where the rental home was. A man she did not know sat down in front of her and asked, "Are you the daughter of Mr so-and-so?" She answered, "Yes." He then told her, "Your father gave me the tax money for your house. Now, please go home."

She returned home praising the Lord for His kindness. She kept thinking about that person and wondering who he was, how he knew her, and the coincidence of meeting him.

The next day she went to St. Mark's Cathedral and attended the liturgy as usual. When she went to get the blessing from St. Pope Kyrillos, he looked at her and said, "I sent St. Mina to pay the money for the house that you were concerned about."

On Spiritual Goodwill

We often fail in vigorously carrying out God's commandments, our spiritual exercises, service commitments, and so many other godly obligations. At times, we are overwhelmed by our failures and weaknesses. We become discouraged as we look back on what is an all too common cycle in our lives. Mother Teresa of Calcutta often taught, and wisely so, that God has called us not to be successful, but to be faithful. The first step in faithfulness is spiritual goodwill.

If God sees even a little goodwill, He will provide abundant help for us with His grace, and will be generously merciful toward us in our failures. Spiritual goodwill is, therefore, related to a pure desire. In the Gospel, the example of Zacchaeus the Tax Collector is a befitting lesson on desire. Zacchaeus "sought to see Who Jesus was" (Lk 19:3). He did not simply want to see Jesus, but who Jesus was. The inference is that Zacchaeus had an honest desire to know more about the Lord Jesus. It was insufficient for him to trust the word of others. And his intense desire led him to do something, as laughable as it might have been to climb up a tree as he did, in order to act upon this desire. And what he did was enough to set in motion his personal conversion and transformation.

Spiritual goodwill is like a seed of salvation in man's heart, upon which God's grace provides the increase. Even before Zacchaeus displayed his desire by climbing the tree, Christ already saw the spiritual goodwill in his heart. He saw the greed in his heart softening and a desire growing with sincerity. Jesus called out those who sought Him with impure intentions and misplaced desires. "Most assuredly, I say to you, you seek Me, not because you saw the signs, but because you ate of the loaves and were filled" (Jn 6:26). St. Augustine asserted that God considers more the purity of the intention of our actions above the actions themselves.

PSALM 56 (57)

"I will seek shelter in the shadow of Your wings until the time of danger has passed"

A priest from Alexandria was suffering from a dangerous disease and was admitted to the hospital, but his condition deteriorated. One night, he went to sleep feeling extremely sad. In his dream, he saw St. Pope Kyrillos VI placing the Cross on his chest exactly on the spot of the pain, saying to him, "Congratulations, Father. I came to facilitate your recovery!" The priest says that when he woke up he felt much better. The doctors recognized that he was fully recovered and discharged him from the hospital.

A week later, the Pope came to the church where the priest served and they celebrated the Divine Liturgy together. When the Liturgy concluded, the priest was amazed to see the Saint put the Cross on his chest and congratulate him for his recovery. He then recalled that it was exactly what he had seen in the dream and he glorified God.

On Spiritual Endurance

In His discourse on the destruction of the Temple and the difficulties of the last days, Jesus taught, "By your patience (endurance) possess your souls" (Lk 21:19). Another translation reads, "By standing firm you will gain life." To endure with patience and firmness means we need to overcome fatigue, stress, or other adverse conditions that we face in a multitude of ways in our life. We cannot grow in any virtue except through being tested against the same virtue. We will not withstand the last days with all its horrors or the deceitful influence the Antichrist will have on the world if we remain unpruned.

Jesus declares to us that the promised rewards are not given to those who begin well, nor those who continue for part of the way, but only those who endure to the end. "A brother asked Abba Sisoes, 'What shall I do, Abba, for I have fallen?' The old man said to him, 'Get up again.' The brother said, 'I have got up again, but I have fallen again.' The old man said, 'Get up again and again.' So then the brother said, 'How many times?' The old man said, 'Until you are taken up either in virtue or in sin. For a man presents himself to judgment in the state in which he is found.'" Clinging to Christ and His Church, nourishing ourselves on His

Word, gaining encouragement from the lives of the saints, will become the fortifying daily bread we need to persevere.

When Jesus explained the Parable of the Sower to the disciples, He emphasized the importance of an enduring and patient heart: "But that which is on rich soil are the ones who, when they have heard the word with a good and upright heart, keep it and yield a harvest through their perseverance" (Lk 8:15). Even if we do not yet have the heroic endurance of the saints, we can grow in this virtue by reducing the time between stalling and beginning again, between falling and rising. Because of our wounded pride, we often remain in prolonged discouragement and sadness. If we humble ourselves, trusting in God's grace and mercy without hesitation, God will crown us with the grace of spiritual endurance.

PSALM 60 (61)

"For You are my refuge, a tower of strength against the enemy"

In 1963, a young man was undergoing his military service in a Special Forces Unit. In May of that year, his unit was selected to go join one of the armed forces fighting in Yemen. In those days, he knew nothing about St. Pope Kyrillos VI except that he was the Patriarch of the church.

While in Yemen, he was exposed to numerous dangers, some that should have ended in death. The fact that he remained intact without a scratch is a great miracle. On one of his missions, he lost his way and found himself wandering between mountains. Suddenly, numerous gunshots were fired directly at him. He lost consciousness and fell to the ground.

Later, when he regained consciousness, he found himself in the hospital. His uniform was shredded and burned but he had no injuries. He later learned from his colleagues that during their night guard duty they saw a moving shadow near them. Thinking it was the enemy, they opened fire. Once they ran out of ammunition, they heard his voice so they rushed over to rescue him and were surprised to find him still alive. They were a group of four people, each with thirty bullets; so about one hundred and twenty bullets were fired at him!

When he returned to Egypt, his younger brother told him that after he left and the family had no news, growing more and more worried and anxious, they went to go see St. Pope Kyrillos and ask for his prayers. When they arrived at the Cathedral of St. Mark, His Holiness was celebrating the evening Vespers service. After the prayers, a large crowd surrounded the Pope as he was on his way out of the church. It was too difficult to reach him. Then they saw His Holiness make his way through the middle of the large crowd and come toward them. He pulled the brother close to himself and, without anyone saying a word, said to him, "Do not fear, your brother will be back soon." The brother was totally shocked at how the Saint knew everything.

On Carrying the Cross

The Cross is the cost of love. It is not the circumstance, person or suffering that is the Cross, but the love that it costs to conquer or transform it. The Cross is not in having the illness, but in the gratitude and patience that accompanies it. The Cross is not in being in a difficult relationship, but in the endurance and self-sacrifice that overcomes it. In Jesus' teaching, the Cross and the cost of discipleship are equated.

The cost of discipleship is a magnanimous, dedicated, and disproportionate love for God above all interests, including family, possessions and one's own life. It is God's love through Christ that sanctifies the wood of the Cross, the sufferings and humiliations of the Cross, not the other way around. Likewise, we do not wait for the Cross, but by loving God and neighbor above our self-interests, we are already under its weight. A great mistake we can make is to think of the Cross as some kind of unique or individual catastrophe, disaster, or hardship. As disciples of Christ, we are called to the chief task of following Him faithfully, obediently, and humbly in the midst of our daily activities.

"I die daily," said St. Paul (1 Co 15:31). The emphasis is on life, not death. Life goes on through death to self, through selfless love. That is why, again, St. Paul could say that he was "put to death all day long" (Ro 8:36, Ps 43:22). The Cross is sought not merely accepted. If suffering is a part of the Cross, it is because it is always a consequence of elevated love. A mother's greatest suffering will always be related to her child, because her child is the greatest object of her love. When God is the object of our love, we will suffer not so much because of circumstances or other people, but because of our own weaknesses and faults that we feel are a hindrance to the consummation of that love.

PSALM 62 (63)

"My soul yearns for You and my body thirsts for You"

A certain man was God-loving from his childhood. Nothing could distract him from his love for God including entertainment or amusements. As a young man, he thought of leaving home and living as a wanderer, carrying no more than his daily bread and worshipping God in an isolated place. He prayed to the Lord to guide him on the way of salvation.

One night after he prayed, he went to sleep on the roof of the house, as was the custom for many Upper Egyptians. He saw in a dream a monk asking him, "Do you want to go to a monastery?" When he answered, "Yes," the monk left and went away. He did not pay much attention to that dream. After one month, the same monk came to him again in a dream and said, "Hurry up and go to the monastery!" When the young man asked him, "Where is that monastery?" the monk did not answer and went away. Again, he did not give much importance to the dream.

After another month, the monk returned and asked, "You haven't gone to the monastery yet? If you don't listen to what I tell you, I will let him punish you." He pointed at someone riding a horse. The young man thought it was the great martyr, Saint George. He asked the monk, "Where do you want me to become a monk?" He answered, "In the monastery of Saint Mina in Old Cairo." He then disappeared. The young man had some doubts which caused him to be very hesitant, since that monastery was not widely known.

He wondered if those dreams were from God or from the devil. But, the image of that monk calling him to monasticism persisted. Fearing punishment from Saint George, whom he had seen riding on his horse, he felt he had no other option but to flee to Cairo. He went to a relative and asked him to show him the way to Saint Mina's Church in Old Cairo. He arrived there at the conclusion of the Sunday Divine Liturgy. He immediately realized that the priest who celebrated the Liturgy was the same monk who had appeared in his dreams three times. It was Fr. Mina the Solitary (the monastic name of St. Pope Kyrillos VI).

The young man did not need to explain anything to the monk as it was clear from the way Fr. Mina looked at him with a big smile. After the

Liturgy, Fr. Mina gave him the blessed bread (*eulogia*) three times, while everyone else received only one. His companion, who brought him to the church, asked why he was laughing. He simply told him that his heart was rejoicing.

After Vespers that evening, Fr. Mina spoke to him, "My son, you have to close all old accounts," which clearly meant he was about to start a new life in that place. He began to tell Fr. Mina how he longed for monasticism. He also told him about Fr. Mina's three visits in his dreams and how he had been in the company of St. George in the last one. Fr. Mina here corrected him saying that his companion had been the Martyr St. Mina, not St. George.

At that point the young man's eyes began to open to see that he was dealing with a saint of that rare type who was guided by the Spirit of God. Fr. Mina said to him, "Congratulations, my son. God willing you shall be a blessing to the monastery!" From then on he began to guide the young man.

On Christian Vocation

Usually, when we think of the word "vocation" in an ecclesiastical sense, we immediately consider priesthood or monasticism. It is certainly true that ministerial priesthood and consecrated life are callings. "And one does not take the honor upon himself, but he is called by God, just as Aaron was" (Heb 5:4). But there is a universal Christian vocation that precedes, and exceeds in importance, these functions in the Church.

God calls all men to union with Him, a life of holiness and sanctification. "For this is the will of God, your sanctification" (1 Th 4:3). This is the only vocation that merits eternal life. One can be a priest or a monk and lose his salvation. These "callings within a calling" are only personally salvific if by carrying out their duties one is united to God, living a holy life.

The early Church Fathers often referred to our baptism as the primal vocation, by which the Christian is called to a total conversion of life. In the baptismal prayers of the Church, the priest prays that the candidate for baptism will be converted from darkness to light, from error to truth, from the ignorance of idolatry to the knowledge of the true God, and from death to life. Further, the prayers instruct that we are called to grow in faith, give glory to God in our life, and to become a temple of the Holy Spirit.

Sanctification is never something for the privileged few. Rather, we should affirm that every state in life can be divine. The Christian vocation is not essentially a call to vacate the situation one is in, but always a summons to live out the very same existence in a new way as a result of the light of Christ and the grace of the Holy Spirit: "let every one lead the life which the Lord has assigned to him, and in which God has called him" (1 Co 7:17).

PSALM 66 (67)

"O God, be gracious to us and bless us and let Your face shine upon us"

A Muslim man from the area of Tanta came to his Christian friend and said, "I have something to ask you but I am a bit embarrassed. I heard about this man of yours [i.e., the Christians] whose name is Pope Kyrillos. I lost two of my cattle. Would he be able to tell me anything about this?"

The Christian friend understood what he was referring to and replied, "Look, he is not someone who looks into a crystal ball or that type of person of which you are thinking!" He answered, "I am sorry. I didn't mean to offend you but please ask him for me."

They went together to the Patriarchate but the Muslim man refused to go inside out of respect. The Christian man went in to see the Pope and told him about his friend's request. The Saint asked, "Why is he always fighting with his neighbors? Tell him to act nicely with people and make peace with his neighbors."

When he told his Muslim friend what the Pope said, he was shocked and asked, "How could he know that? I didn't even tell you!" Two weeks later he returned to his Christian friend with a large amount of poultry and about one hundred eggs and said, "Do whatever you want with these but don't say I brought them. After I made peace with my neighbors, my cattle were returned to me. This man of yours, Pope Kyrillos, is tall with a long beard. He came to me in a dream and blessed the return of my cattle." His gifts were delivered to St. Mina's Monastery.

On Generosity of Spirit

Jesus often used images from farming and agriculture in His teachings. This is not surprising given most of His listeners were either farmers or very familiar with agricultural life. In the Parable of the Sower (Mt 13:1-9), God's generosity is being displayed. Seeds are scattered everywhere in abundance. "I have come that they may have life, and have it in abundance" (Jn 10:10). In fact, by His Passion, Death, and Resurrection, Jesus shows that His love has no bounds.

As Jesus vindicates God's love toward mankind, so also does He long for us to justify His sacrificial love before others through our own generous love. "As the Father has sent Me, I also send you" (Jn 20:21). Often, we think of generosity only in terms of money, possessions or time. But generosity of spirit is not about these things; it is about being generous in my goodwill toward others, about a growing desire to sow goodness all around me. The spiritually generous always feels they are not able to do enough for their family, church or community, and they look for opportunities to practice sacrifice without expecting anything in return. They receive more satisfaction from giving than from receiving, placing all their expectations in "the surpassing worth of knowing Christ Jesus our Lord" (Php 3:8).

Generosity of spirit is Christian nobility: "But the ones that fell on the good ground are those who, having heard the word with a noble and good heart, keep it and bear fruit with patience" (Lk 8:15). Elder Paisios of Mount Athos says that such a person "rises above" earthly logic and justice. Such a person gladly relinquishes his rights in this life for the sake of the Gospel and the love of God. St. Paul writes, "Remember this: if you sow sparingly, you will reap sparingly, and if you sow generously, you will reap generously as well" (2 Co 9:6).

PSALM 69 (70)

"Make haste, O God, to rescue me; O Lord, come quickly to my aid"

A certain father received a letter from his daughter which deeply upset him. In it, his daughter complained about a conspiracy against her husband. One of his colleagues falsely accused him of wrongdoing and as a result he was removed from his duties. The matter was extremely embarrassing to him and caused him great distress. He was at a loss for what to do.

Taking the letter, the father went to the new Cathedral to seek the blessings of the Apostle St. Mark and St. Reweis. Walking up the front stairs, he heard a car honk. He saw it was St. Pope Kyrillos VI getting out of his car. He was on his way to pray the Vespers Raising of Incense. He went down to meet the Pope, bowed and kissed his hand. They went up the stairs together with the Saint's left hand on his shoulder until they reached the Sanctuary.

During Vespers, the Pope asked him to read the Holy Gospel. When he finished the reading and went to kiss the Pope's hand, the Pope asked him, "What's in your pocket? God will take care of everything!"

The man was surprised that the Saint knew what was in his pocket before he even had a chance to talk to him about it. It was the letter his daughter sent him!

The Saint did not say another word about it, and the father did not expect him to, as he knew the value of each word and its power in action. Later, he received another letter from his daughter, this time bearing good news - the painful trial ended by the manifestation of the truth and, as such, joy returned by the word of the Saint's pure mouth.

On God's Comfort

One of the most touching dialogues between Christ and His disciples takes place in the Upper Room on Holy Thursday. We can only imagine the tension; Jesus is about to be betrayed, arrested, tried, and crucified. The Gospel tells us that He Himself is "deeply troubled" (Jn 13:21) and knows that His hour has come (Jn 12:23). The disciples likewise are confused; Christ just spoke to them of His impending departure from them, His passion, betrayal and Peter's thrice denial. In all of this, Christ turns His attention to comforting His disciples (Jn 14:1).

When our hearts are troubled, it can quickly begin to feel like our life is a downward spiral. Feelings of isolation, powerlessness, grief, and despair can overtake us. I imagine that the hearts of the disciples were likewise overcome by these feelings. "Let not your heart be troubled; you believe in God, believe also in Me" (Jn 14:1). Another translation reads, "You place your trust in God. Trust also in Me." The Lord does not offer the disciples any promise that their future problems will go away. Rather, He asks them to "place their trust" in Him. He wants us to tether our hearts to His heart. "Take My yoke upon you... For My yoke is easy and My burden is light" (Mt 11:29, 30).

We often falter because we work alone, relying on our own resources. There is no difficulty for which God does not have a solution. Even if at times it seems we have been left alone, it is only to arouse in us a greater confidence. The disciples were often put to the test. But little by little they arrived at the realization that the only person they could stake all their lives on was Christ. "But Simon Peter answered Him, "Lord, to whom shall we go? You have the words of eternal life" (Jn 6:68). In the times your heart is troubled, remember that Jesus turns to you, as He did the disciples on Holy Thursday, and comforts you with the promise that He is worthy and capable of being trusted.

PSALM 83 (84)

"My heart and my flesh cry out for the living God"

A student who lived in the student's quarters annexed to the Church of St. Mina in Old Cairo was preoccupied by thoughts of atheism and communist ideology. He spent many nights awake and torn between his studies and those thoughts which disturbed his mind and life. He felt like he was drowning in those thoughts.

One night he was very stressed and came close to the decision of completely denying God. He was awake until 1:00 a.m. and when he went to the window to look toward Fr. Mina's [St. Pope Kyrillos'] room he saw the light still on. So he said to himself, "I will go and knock once. If he is still awake, I will go in and talk with him. But if he is asleep, I will wait until the morning."

He knocked at the door and Fr. Mina opened and invited him upstairs. The student then said, "When I sat with Fr. Mina I lost all interest in those atheistic thoughts; but I still let him know what I was going through. I told him about the thoughts which haunted me and described the state that I reached.

"Strangely, Fr. Mina did not engage in discussing those ideas. However, he said a few words and then prayed for me. After his prayer, I felt many ties and bonds on me had been undone and I was greatly comforted. I didn't know where the thoughts that troubled me before had gone as they were completely wiped out and never came back to my mind."

On Thoughts

The ministry of Christ was one of teaching and healing, but also one of exposing. "For nothing is secret that will not be revealed, nor anything hidden that will not be known and come to light" (Lk 8:17). Our thoughts are important; they are significant to our own interior well-being and they are important to God. When the Lord rebuked the Scribes and Pharisees, it was not for any crimes or moral offenses but because their thoughts were evil. "But Jesus, knowing their thoughts, said, 'Why do you think evil in your hearts?'" (Mt 9:4).

If we think in terms of cause and effect, evil thoughts are the cause, and sinful acts are the effect. And likewise, good and noble thoughts produce good effects in us and around us. Thoughts are the seeds and our words and actions are the fruit. Just as one of the saints pointed out, a snake is not only poisonous when it bites, but still contains the poison in itself when it does not bite. The battlefield of the Christian life begins with our thoughts. Jesus taught that the Kingdom of God is within us (Lk 17:21) but also warned that "if a kingdom is divided against itself, that kingdom cannot stand" (Mk 3:24).

A secular article some years ago suggested that the average person has approximately 70,000 thoughts per day. We can certainly surmise that most of these thoughts are negative thoughts on the past or future, and not ones of faith, hope, and love. The two most common counsels of the saints on dealing with thoughts are to ignore them or to replace them. To ignore our thoughts is to not give them too much attention or importance, neither to be surprised by them nor dwell on them. One spiritual father likened it to a puppy dog vying for your attention while you are immersed in an important conversation with someone. We can always replace the bad thought with a good thought or with a short prayer. The Jesus Prayer or verses from the Psalms are perfect for these moments.

We must not be tempted to place all the weight of the spiritual life on our words and actions, but discern that our thoughts are the foundation of everything. And on the Last Day, "He will bring to light what is hidden in darkness and will expose the motives of the heart. At that time each will receive their praise from God" (1 Co 4:5).

PSALM 84 (85)

"Show us Your mercy, O Lord, and grant us Your salvation"

When Fr. Mina was selected by the Church to become the next Patriarch, a certain lady made a sarcastic comment about his inadequacy for the position.

One morning, when this lady was giving her sick son his medicinal injections, she made a mistake, injuring her son which caused him severe inflammation and a massive growth at the injection site. After surgical consultation with a doctor, the mother was told that her son had to undergo an operation to alleviate the inflammation.

Feeling guilty and depressed about her son's situation, the mother decided to go visit the new Pope and ask him for a prayer. When she met with him, she confessed to the Saint the sarcastic comments she made when he was first chosen. She expressed her extreme regret and sorrow for what she said. The Saint, in his great mercy, unconditionally forgave her, and then prayed for her and her son. He gave her a piece of cotton anointed with holy oil and instructed her to place it on the boy's injury. The very next morning, not only was all the inflammation gone, but the original illness the boy had been suffering from, which necessitated the injections in the first place, had also been miraculously cured.

On Divine Mercy

Often, the words "mercy" and "compassion" are used interchangeably. Compassion means to "suffer with," and is derived from two Latin words: com, meaning with; and pati meaning suffer. The root of the word "mercy," however, is related to "reward" or "wages." It implies one is in a position of power or some form of disparity. Masters were to be merciful to servants, and the rich to the poor. From a human point of view, then, one can show mercy without feeling compassionate. It is also true that one can feel compassionate and pity another, but not act in a merciful way.

Christ revealed to us the heart of the Father, Who is always mercifully compassionate and compassionately merciful. He acts but also feels, suffers and journeys with us in our misery. "And when Jesus went out He saw a great multitude; and He was moved with compassion for them, and healed their sick" (Mt 14:14). Jesus is moved in His interior, and then acts to remedy. If God's "love" seeks all that is good for us, then His "mercy" seeks to remedy and alleviate all that afflicts us. God's mercy is directed at our liberation from death, sin, and the devil. He raises us to divine adoption into God's family and gives us the promise of eternal glory and bliss.

Jesus' mercy contrasts God's heart with the hard and scornful hearts of the Pharisees who complained that Jesus "welcomes sinners and eats with them" (Lk 15:2). The mercy of God is a bridge that dissolves the distance separating our utter unworthiness from His divine life and eternal glory. As one of the saints stated, He is the God of those who are miserable. And because His mercy is eternal and boundless, so must our confidence in Him also be without limits. The more wretched and weak we find ourselves, the more of a right we have to His mercy. "Let us therefore come boldly to the throne of grace, that we may obtain mercy and find grace to help in time of need" (Heb 4:16).

PSALM 85 (86)

"Save Your servant who puts his trust in You"

On August 18 1960, Saint Pope Kyrillos VI visited the Virgin Mary's Monastery in Assiut (El-Muharraq Monastery). The personal driver for the bishop of Assiut was entrusted with the responsibility of looking after His Holiness in the guest house. He was instructed not to leave the Saint's side for any reason at all.

When His Holiness arrived, the driver was surprised that the Pope knew his name. During this visit, the driver's brother-in-law came to tell him that his wife was suffering from postnatal fever, and the doctors were beginning to lose hope for her condition. She wanted to see and talk to her husband about their 19-day-old daughter. But he could not abandon his duty serving His Holiness.

The Pope noticed that he was worried, although he did not say a word to him, and turned to him and said, "Do not be afraid, she is not going to die." He answered, "Pray for her, Your Holiness." The Saint asked him to bring water and oil; he then prayed on both and told him to take them home. His wife drank from the water and anointed herself with the oil. At that time, her condition was very critical. A change occurred in his wife immediately. She opened her eyes and asked for food. She stopped taking the medications and was perfectly well again.

On the Mystery of Suffering

One of the saints remarked that while we are destined for Mount Tabor (glory), we are formed on Mount Calvary (suffering). While suffering will always be wrapped in mystery, it is rooted in the dogmatic truths of our faith. Man was made for "incorruption." In the Garden of Eden, Adam was in harmony with God, with himself, with Eve and with the rest of creation. All this harmony was disrupted as a result of sin and subsequent corruption. God's intervention to redeem us, through the Incarnation, Death and Resurrection of Jesus Christ, restored man's relationship with God, conquered the enemies of sin, death, and evil, and opened to us the path of perfection. But as exhibited in the experience of God's own humanity through the Passion of Christ, suffering remained a reality.

Though suffering persists, it is no longer meaningless or pointless. By displaying through the Cross that the greatest evil resulted in the greatest good for the entire human race, God has both opened infinite possibilities for suffering's greater good, but also hidden its meaning except to those who look upon Him with faith and simplicity. "At that time Jesus answered and said, "I thank You, Father, Lord of heaven and earth, that You have hidden these things from the wise and prudent and have revealed them to babes" (Mt 11:25).

Ultimately, the answer to our own sufferings is a gift of God to the soul in the intimacy of a personal relationship sustained by love. Much will remain a mystery wrapped in darkness until we enter the presence of God. "For now we see in a mirror dimly, but then face to face. Now I know in part; then I shall understand fully, even as I have been fully understood" (1 Co 13:12). But this does not mean that we cannot extrapolate some general understandings of the usefulness of suffering. From the Scriptures and the lives of the saints, we know that suffering can be utilized to awaken us, test us, humble us, and purify us.

PSALM 86 (87)

"The dwelling of all who rejoice is within You"

An army lieutenant was far from God since his youth, spending the prime of his life in prodigal living. He heard about Fr. Mina the Solitary (St. Pope Kyrillos VI) and that he was a righteous and devout man. The young man felt an inclination to go and confess with him. The officer spent one hour confessing all the sins of his youth while Fr. Mina listened without saying a word. Then, the officer started to feel an intense heat and his body began sweating. When he finished his confession, Fr. Mina asked him:

"And now my son, what do you intend to do?"

"To repent, Father."

"May God absolve you."

"Can I have Communion?"

"Yes, you can."

Fr. Mina prayed the absolution and the young man left wondering why he did not reprimand him or impose any penance on him. He felt deep sorrow and contrition. The next day he went to the church but could not bring himself to approach for Holy Communion. Fr. Mina asked him why he did not partake of the Mystery and when he told him he just could not, Fr. Mina gave a word of encouragement and instructed him to approach the following week.

Week after week for over a month he repeated the same scenario. Afterwards, whenever he confessed to Fr. Mina, he would ask him, "And what do you intend to do?" His answer was, "to repent." Then Fr. Mina would reply, "May God absolve you," but every time he left him he felt as if Fr. Mina had given him a very hard lesson or slapped him across the face a times, as every time he came out crying bitterly. In that way Fr. Mina was able to change his life, not by a lecture or a rebuke, but by a concealed spiritual power through love and compassion.

On the Reasons for Suffering

Suffering exists in every aspect of our human experience and can impact us at physical, psychological, emotional or spiritual levels. Through the examples given to us in Holy Scripture and the lives of the saints, we can generalize some meanings and purposes given to our sufferings. We have to approach the mystery of suffering always attempting to see God's perspective, in which the eternal, heavenly, and incorruptible implications always outweigh temporal, earthly, and corruptible goods. "For what is your life? It is even a vapor that appears for a little time and then vanishes away" (Jas 4:14).

The first benefit we gain from suffering is that it awakens us from the sleep-walking of earthly life and all its enticing pleasures. A pertinent example here is that of the Prodigal Son. The suffering of his miserable condition awakened in him the memory of his father's home and a desire to abandon the foolishness of his plans and return. Suffering sometimes is the only way that we "come to ourselves" (Lk 15:17) and return to God in repentance and conversion of life.

The second benefit is that suffering tests us and raises us to a higher, even heroic, level of virtue. Job is the classic example. But we can also look at the disciples and find in their experiences the many opportunities they had to prove whether their faith and love for Christ was simply utilitarian or a pure love for God.

The third benefit of suffering is that it disciplines and humbles us in this life, freeing us from judgement in the next life. God never judges twice! "But when we are judged, we are chastened by the Lord, that we may not be condemned with the world" (1 Co 11:32). As hard as it may seem and feel while we are in the midst of the suffering itself, the Lord's chastening is a sign of His great love for us. "For the Lord disciplines the one He loves, and chastises every son whom He receives" (Heb 12:6).

Finally, suffering is evangelical, manifesting the love of God and His redemption to the world. "Now I rejoice in my sufferings for your sake" (Col 1:24), St. Paul wrote to the Church in Colossae, revealing how believers prolong and declare the paschal Mystery of Christ's Death and Resurrection, by uniting their own trials and suffering to His.

PSALM 90 (91)

"You are my refuge and my fortress, my God in whom I place my trust"

One lady admired St. Pope Kyrillos VI very much and used to visit him regularly. She was diagnosed with breast cancer and was under the care of many doctors, including her two sons who were surgeons. There was no other treatment other than surgery.

She felt compelled to send her sister to St. Pope Kyrillos. When the Pope saw her, he called her by name and asked about her sister's case before being informed of anything. When she told him about her sister's condition, the Saint said to her, "Your sister is well. I will send St. Mina to her tonight." He then gave her some cotton anointed with holy oil and told her to anoint her sister with it.

That night, she was able to enter into a deep sleep, confident of the words of the Saint knowing his close relationship with St. Mina.

At about 2:00 a.m., she was awakened when a bright light filled her room and she saw three young physicians standing next to her bed. The most senior among them had an indescribable radiance around his head. She heard him giving instructions to his assistants, including to give an injection in her arm.

When everything ended, she fell asleep again until 5:00 a.m. When she awoke, she found bandages around her breast. She woke up her sister and her sons who also witnessed it and they were all amazed. When her physicians who were going to operate on her examined her, they concluded that a successful operation had already been performed on her.

On the Meaning of Watchfulness

On the night before the tenth and final plague inflicted upon the Egyptians, the death of their first-born, the Lord declared that He would "keep watch" over them (Ex 12:42) as He brought them across the Red Sea. The Lord keeps a constant vigil over our lives, leading us and protecting us until He brings us to our eternal homeland. The Israelites were instructed to keep an annual vigil during the Passover in remembrance of God's vigilance on their behalf.

In the Garden of Gethsemane on the night of Jesus' arrest and the beginning of His Passion, knowing His time was near, He said to His disciples, "My soul is overwhelmed with sorrow to the point of death. Stay here and keep watch with Me" (Mt 26:38). The disciples fell asleep. In deep agony, the Lord returned again to His disciples and said, "Could you not keep watch with Me for one hour?" (Mt 26:40). And again, they fell asleep. We can only imagine how, later, the disciples would regret not keeping watch with their Master and friend. It seems the Church transferred the concept of an all-night vigil, a time of keeping watch with the Lord, to certain feasts throughout the ecclesiastical calendar.

The Greek word *Paramoni* (*Baramoun*), meaning to "keep watch," is what a watchman does. In the Church, it consists of an intense feeling of anticipation before a feast, what all of our preparations have been leading us to. We can think of Holy Week, building up to Great Friday, immediately leading into the all-night vigil of Bright Saturday, all in preparation for the great joy of the Feast of the Resurrection. Indeed, every feast is a reminder that our lives are a constant "*paramoni*" in preparation for that final and eternal celebration of the Kingdom of God. Watchfulness is not a ritual relegated to the day before a feast or a season in the Church, but must be an essential interior disposition in the mind and heart of each Christian.

PSALM 92 (93)

"Your throne is prepared from the beginning; You are from everlasting"

A friend of the clerical secretary at the Patriarchal Cathedral came and asked for an appointment to see His Holiness Pope Kyrillos VI because his wife was very ill. As a newly ordained priest, the clerical secretary wanted to add more reverence to the way people came to meet His Holiness, so he asked his friend to return in a week to see the Pope.

Later, when the Saint saw the priest, he looked at him intensely and said, "My son, the man told you that his wife was ill and you gave him an appointment for a week from now?! Call and have him come immediately. Tell him that His Holiness is waiting for him." The priest tried to argue, but His Holiness insisted saying, "Right now!" He called the man who came immediately with his wife.

When the priest went to tell the Pope that they had arrived, he already knew and asked him to let them in to see him. The priest walked in with them and found St. Pope Kyrillos sitting on his chair and holding the Cross in his hand. As the husband started to approach the Pope, he fell down on his face. He got up and walked another two steps but then fell again. This happened three times before he finally reached the Pope. When the man was about to tell His Holiness about his wife's illness, the Pope said, "My son, do not say anything." After raising the Cross over his wife's head and praying, His Holiness told him, "That is all. She is not sick anymore." Indeed, she was healed on the spot.

When they were leaving, the priest asked the man why earlier he had fallen down three times. He told him that he saw Pope Kyrillos sitting on his chair and his eyes emitted a wonderful radiance like the sun and his face was illuminated with a very strong light. As he approached him, the light became brighter and brighter and this repeated three times. He said to the priest, "Who can stare at the sun? That is why I fell down."

On the Essence of Watchfulness

The essence of watchfulness in the spiritual life is not in prolonged physical worship, fasting, or other forms of external asceticism, but the inner watchfulness, or vigilance, of the heart. "What comes out of a man, that defiles a man. For from within, out of the heart of men, proceed evil thoughts, adulteries, fornications, murders, thefts, covetousness, wickedness, deceit, lewdness, an evil eye, blasphemy, pride, foolishness. All these evil things come from within and defile a man" (Mk 7:20-23).

The heart is the innermost being of man, the deep place of encounter between the Spirit of God and man's spirit. Since the Kingdom of God is within us, vigilance concentrates our attention to His presence and safeguards the heart to remain in harmony with God. This also explains the importance of living in the present moment, for if our attention is not on God's presence and movements within us, the visitation of divine grace passes us by.

Watchfulness teaches us discernment, for just as a watchman recognizes an imposing threat or an approaching enemy, the heart learns to recognize and reject evil thoughts. One of the saints taught that spiritual maturity is measured not by feelings it experiences in loving God, but in vigilant watchfulness to avoid sin. The state of watchfulness is not, however, simply a defensive or passive state, but one that actively occupies the mind and the heart, keeping it centered on Christ and the Heavenly Kingdom.

A priest who was imprisoned and tortured in a Romanian communist prison recalled another much beloved priest who was a great consolation to many of the Christian prisoners. When the prisoners were allowed to walk outside in the garden, this priest would ask one of the other prisoners for their story. The person would usually take the time to complain about the communists and their evils. But the priest, after listening attentively, would reply, "You've said plenty about the Communists; now tell me about yourself. When did you confess last?"

The Ninth Hour

PSALM 95 (96)

"For great is the Lord and worthy of all praise"

A certain lady was blessed to work in Cairo near St. Mark's Cathedral and attend the daily Divine Liturgies with St. Pope Kyrillos VI. Her father was suffering from prostatitis and was unable to urinate for three days. She went to the Patriarchate and waited in the upstairs reception room, surprised that there were no other visitors there at all. Suddenly, the Saint opened the door and said, "Come my daughter, what do you want? I heard a voice telling me to open the door. God will grant you your wish."

She told him about her father's sickness and the Saint responded, "He will recover." She lowered her head and he prayed one of the psalms followed by another prayer.

She traveled to Fayoum on the same day and found that her father had recovered. He was finally able to urinate and they learned it was at the same time when the Saint was praying for him.

On Personal Prayer - Recitative Prayer

The most familiar form of personal prayer is verbal, or recitative prayer. It consists of the Lord's Prayer, Psalms, and other pre-written prayers contained in prayer books, mostly composed by the great saints of previous generations. Through them we are trained in the language of prayer, developing a spirit of prayer. A child first learns the letters of the alphabet, then small words independent of each other, then sentences, until they succeed in reading complete books in varying levels of difficulty. With each step, the child's freedom expands.

In the same way, in the life of the Spirit, we need to learn a spiritual manner of communication, not in the choice or excellence of the words per se, but in the spirit, sentiments, and dispositions contained in pure prayer. The Lord Jesus often withdrew to pray, and on one such occasion, the disciples observing Him in deep prayer, must have been moved by the intimacy of His converse with the Father. They asked Him, "'Lord, teach us to pray.'...So He said to them, 'When you pray, say...'" (Lk 11:1, 2). The Lord's Prayer is thus connected with the Prayer of Jesus, Himself. It is not simply reciting a formula but an elevated movement of the soul toward God.

The Psalms are especially sublime because they are both words inspired by the Holy Spirit Himself, as well as words expressed from the perspective of a human heart crying out to God within the human experience and through human sentiments. In a sense, then, by use of the Psalms, we speak to God with His own words; they are themselves the very language of God. We must always remain vigilant in times of recitative prayer that we are first recollected in God's presence, directing our hearts and affections toward Him, so that we do not fall victim to mechanical recitation.

PSALM 96 (97)

"The Lord preserves the souls of His saints; He will deliver them"

On the Feast of Resurrection in 1965, St. Pope Kyrillos VI was in St. Mina's monastery in Mariut. He was carrying so many problems that could only be described as bitter. His heart was heavy with sadness. He asked the monks to turn off all the lights (generators), satisfied with only the lights from the candles. His tears kept falling, coming down on the Holy Eucharist, and he kept trying to stop them but was not successful.

The Divine Liturgy was very long; it ended at 3:30 a.m., and after the Liturgy he said to his disciple, "Did you see the visitors who were in the church, my son?" He answered, "Where were they, my Father? For, Your Holiness had ordered all visitors to leave the monastery this morning." He said, "I don't mean those visitors, but the church was so full that there was no place for another to enter, and they were the ones who asked me to turn off the lights."

His Holiness left the church comforted after God had sent these saints to him. It was when he saw them that his tears increased. Without a doubt, they had lifted their hearts to the heavens, asking for the peace of the Church and most of the problems were solved a few days later.

On Personal Prayer - Meditative Prayer

As the soul progresses in the spiritual life, it feels the need for prayer that is more interior and intimate. Meditative prayer is a framework for more personal conversation with the Lord through the use of sacred texts. Through the use of the Holy Scriptures, especially the Gospel, and devotional texts from the saints and other masters in the spiritual life, meditative prayer is an interactive exercise. St. Paul writes, "Finally, brethren, let your minds be filled with whatever is true, whatever is honorable, whatever is just, whatever is pure, whatever is pleasing, whatever is commendable, whatever is excellent, whatever is worthy of praise..." (Php 4:8).

One spiritual master compared meditative prayer to the way birds drink water. Birds will first bend their heads toward the water filling their bill with a few drops, then tilt their head back toward the sky, using gravity to send the water into their digestive tract, and then repeat the process. We should choose a text that arouses devotion, avoiding philosophical or speculative writings. In meditation, the focus is on prayer not simply learning. It is an exercise of love, more than the work of the mind. St. John Chrysostom says that meditating through spiritual reading will ensure that we will always be filled and have a firm foundation in God.

The first step is to nourish the mind with thoughts about God by reading; the second is to reflect, ponder, and digest such thoughts; the third is to speak to God in our own words with those thoughts. It is a movement from the mind to the heart. The heart is "activated" by the mind's engagement with the text. Movements of gratitude, praise, contrition, repentance, faith, hope and love within the heart are indications that we moved from the first step to the second. The third step is a simple loving conversation with the One Who has invited us into His presence.

Finally, after converse with God from our meditation, we should spend some moments in silence and stillness. "Be still, and know that I am God" (Ps 45:10). This is a time when we stop "doing" and learn to just "be" in God's presence and receive from Him the peace "which surpasses all understanding" (Php 4:7).

PSALM 97 (98)

"The Lord has made known His salvation; He has manifested His righteousness for all the nations to see"

From 1962 to 1964, the youth of the Church of the Virgin Mary at Maadi used to visit St. Pope Kyrillos VI every Thursday after Vespers, to receive his blessing and ask for his prayers. They were always welcomed and the Saint was always happy to receive them.

On one occasion, a young man was with them who suffered from epilepsy since his childhood. However, his treatment was ineffective. As the group was waiting in the reception room on the ground floor, the young man had an epileptic seizure and collapsed in violent convulsions. All those present at the time crowded around him and tried to revive him; at the same time, the Pope was coming down from his cell.

The Saint asked them to carry the young man to a sofa. He placed the Cross on the young man's forehead and called his name (although he had not been told of his name), and the young man responded to the Pope. He regained consciousness, opened his eyes, and looked around. The Saint pressed his hand against the young man's forehead and said with a gentle smile, "No, no, you are all right."

This happened in January 1963 and since then the young man enjoyed good health and never had any more seizures.

On Personal Prayer - Contemplative Prayer

There are three main types of prayer: recitative, meditative, and contemplative. But contemplative prayer is the least structured and ritualistic of these. In fact, there is no single or easy definition for contemplative prayer, because it is the unique expression of silent love between God and the soul. What, perhaps, distinguishes contemplative prayer most from the other two is that God takes a greater initiative to seize our heart. On our part, without words or texts, we look at Him Who is looking at us. That does not mean forming a mental image of God, but rather a look of faith and love to the One Whose attention never leaves us.

The famous 19th century French priest, John Vianney, questioned a peasant who, day after day, sat in the back of the church for hours looking at the Cross without words or gestures. The priest asked him what he was doing. His response was, "I look at Him and He looks at me, and both of us are happy." Through contemplation, we learn the love language of silence, which St. Isaac the Syrian called the "language of the age to come." Due to an intense love, words become insufficient and the Holy Spirit Himself intercedes for us "with groanings which cannot be uttered" (Ro 8:26). And in the silence, God listens to the longing deep within our souls.

We are tempted to minimize the importance of contemplative prayer since, unlike verbal prayer and meditation, it is more difficult to measure that we have actually accomplished something. But spiritual theology, through the experience of the saints, affirms that contemplative prayer is a high and exalted degree, or stage, of prayer. One of the saints said that the soul's profit is not in thinking much, but in loving much. Through contemplative prayer, we discover the great privilege of our filial relationship with our Heavenly Father, that His gaze is always on us, that His presence is within us, and that we can always find Him waiting for us.

PSALM 98 (99)

"Exalt the Lord our God and worship at His footstool; for He is Holy"

A certain lady often visited St. Pope Kyrillos VI to receive his blessings, knowing how holy he was and how much he helped those in need. When she learned her niece was in a certain kind of trouble, she suggested that her niece ask the Saint for his blessing. Instead, her niece decided to go to one of the charlatans in the city of Luxor. He gave her a potion to drink every morning. Because she was convinced that her troubles would be solved this way, she woke up early every morning to drink the liquid.

The family finally convinced her to go see St. Pope Kyrillos VI. When they arrived there, they quietly bowed in front of the Saint and asked for his blessing. He blessed the other family members with his hand Cross, but he compelled the girl to kneel and prayed for her for a long time. As soon as they got home, she vomited the liquid that she had taken that morning. Since that time, her problems disappeared and she learned that she should ask the Lord through the intercessions of the saints for her problems.

On the Four Degrees of Love - 1st & 2nd Degrees

Bernard of Clairvaux was a famous abbot of a monastery at Clairvaux, France in the 11th century. In his work, *The Love of God,* he presents a beautiful image of progression in the spiritual life by means of four degrees of love. These four degrees are both instructive and useful for times of reflection and meditation. The four degrees are: 1) loving yourself for your own sake (selfish love); 2) loving God for your own sake (dependent love); 3) loving God for His own sake (intimate love); and 4) loving yourself for God's sake (unitive love).

The first degree of love is not properly a love for God at all since it is a purely natural and selfish disposition. "The natural body came first, and then the spiritual" (1 Co 15:6). It is like an infant coming out of the womb that can only be nursed, unaware of anyone else. Soon though, we begin to realize how dependent we are on God and others. Usually, what causes this is life's difficulties and the realization that depending on others facilitates satisfying my own needs and desires. The Spirit leads us to hear God's voice saying, "Without Me you can do nothing" (Jn 15:5).

The second degree of love, then, is when we begin to comprehend God's graciousness. That He is the Lover of Mankind and that "every good gift and every perfect gift is from above, and comes down from the Father of lights" (Jas 1:17). Yet, it is still love for your own benefit, not God's own sake. We are motivated by receiving from God–whether blessings, gifts, favors, assistance, forgiveness, or the like. In such ways we approach God like a sort of divine, vending machine. Nonetheless, this stage puts us in contact with God through worship, prayer, and the Mysteries (Sacraments). As God's grace works in us, drawing us more and more, we come to "taste and see how good is the Lord" (Ps 33:8). We are then led to the third degree.

PSALM 99 (100)

"His kindness endures forever, and His faithfulness is constant to all generations"

In 1968, there was a much-loved priest who St. Pope Kyrillos VI relocated to the Patriarchate for six months to serve closely alongside him. The whole parish (unaware as to why) rose in something of an uprising. All those in Sunday School, youth groups, and the church committee would ask, "How could you remove this beloved priest?" The people began cursing. Buses overflowing with people arrived at the Patriarchate. "We want our priest back!", they screamed.

After six months, the Saint moved him to another far more sought-after parish. Once more, the uprising took place, with cursing and intense criticism. And yet the Saint remained silent. This went on for some time, until an old friend from Pope Kyrillos' time in Old Cairo rebuked him, "You are causing trouble, everyone is disturbed and angry; just return the priest to his parish! Do we need more troubles?" The Saint calmly confided to his dear friend, "If you only knew the reality, this priest is not worthy of the priesthood."

Not worthy of priesthood? And yet he stayed silent for six months, being mocked, criticized, sworn at, and not once did the Saint open his mouth to explain. It was not that the priest simply made a mistake; he was not worthy of priesthood at all. Yet St. Pope Kyrillos received him in his bosom, in the Patriarchate, and then returned him healed to a far more sought-after parish than the first. The Saint knew the priest's mistakes–which we may imagine were scandalous in the least–and yet he loved and healed the priest, regardless of the personal cost.

On the Four Degrees of Love - 3rd & 4th Degrees

The third degree of love, according to Bernard of Clairvaux, is intimate love; loving God for His own sake. From the degree of dependency in the second stage, we begin to taste the sweetness of Divine Grace and intimacy with the Lord. Being in the presence of God is blissful for its own sake and one begins to forget all the many requests and needs of an earthly nature, desiring more and more to love God because He is worthy of such love. "We love Him because He first loved us" (1 Jn 4:19).

It might seem that we have reached the summit of love, for what can be more noble than loving God purely for God's sake? Certainly, God's majesty elicits honor, praise, and adoration, and our happiness in eternity will be in offering these with the angels. But God's love is the love of a Father, not merely enjoying intimacy with His children but rejoicing in their exaltation, in receiving all that is His. "Son, you are always with me, and all that I have is yours" (Lk 15:31). Bernard of Clairvaux describes the fourth degree as unitive love–loving yourself for God's sake. This is why God created us and redeemed us, to give us a share of His own glory. "Now, therefore, you are no longer strangers and foreigners, but fellow citizens with the saints and members of the household of God" (Eph 2:19).

In the High Priestly Prayer (Jn 17), Jesus intercedes for us with the Father whereby He opens His heart before us, revealing to us the sublime calling of humanity:

> "I do not pray for these alone, but also for those who will believe in Me through their word; that they all may be one, as You, father, are in Me, and I in You; that they also may be one in Us, that the world may believe that You sent Me. And the glory which You gave Me I have given them, that they may be one just as We are one: I in them, and You in Me; that they may be made perfect in one, and that the world may know that You have sent Me, and have loved them as You have loved Me. Father, I desire that they also whom You gave Me may be with Me where I am, that they may behold My glory which You have given Me; for You loved Me before the foundation of the world" (Jn 17:20-24).

PSALM 100 (101)

"I will walk in the path of blamelessness; when will You come to me?"

In 1991, a priest who had known St. Pope Kyrillos VI since the days he was a monk in Old Cairo, suffered from sun stroke, meningitis and malaria His temperature reached 42 °C (107 °F) and the pains he suffered were utterly unbearable. For two months, he had no sleep and immediately vomited anything he ate. Because of the intense pain, he wished for death to come. He blamed St. Pope Kyrillos VI for abandoning him all this time.

One night while unable to sleep, the Saint came to him wearing his white priestly vestments and a crown on his head. He asked, "What is wrong?" The priest answered, "I have been sick in bed and you abandoned me! I am dying. Either ask God to heal me or bring an end to my life." The Saint said, "Do not worry. God is with you." He crossed him three times and added, "By God's will, and through the blessings of St. Mina the Wonderworker, you will be cured and there will be no trace of the disease left." The priest tried to sit up to greet him but he was already gone. He cried, "Wait, Your Holiness, wait until I greet you!" Those around him heard him say this but thought he was delirious and about to die. They asked him what happened but he did not respond.

After, he fell into a deep and uninterrupted sleep for twelve hours after two sleepless months. When he woke up, the pains were gone. He asked for something to eat and the food remained in his stomach. He realized he had been healed by the prayers of St. Pope Kyrillos VI and his great intercessor St. Mina. All the family and friends who had been expecting his death at any moment were astonished.

On Asceticism

God created children, not slaves. Being created in His image and likeness, we are endowed with rationality and freedom. Only in coming into existence out of non-existence does man have no say. But, as St. Augustine indicated, God will not justify us without our cooperation. The entirety of the spiritual life depends on this synergy between God's grace and man's free will. This does not mean that the two are equal, for God's part is infinitely greater than man's, but without man's minimal contribution, it is impossible to be sanctified and saved. "For we are God's coworkers" (1 Co 3:9).

The word "asceticism" often suggests a practice of mortifying, if not punishing the body. This view is not only incomplete but could very well lead to a heretical notion of dualism between body and soul in a way which sees the body as evil. "Asceticism" in Greek simply means "exercise" or "training," as in the exercise or training of an athlete. It refers primarily to the struggle against the sinful passions (pride, anger, lust, envy, etc.) and the acquisition of the virtues through spiritual exercises and activities that attract the grace of God. It is often referred to as spiritual combat or spiritual warfare.

Though it might seem like a minor nuance, the distinction is critical: man does not earn God's grace, he prepares for it. Man cannot muscle his way into salvation. "Unless the LORD builds the house, they labor in vain who build it; unless the LORD guards the city, the watchman stays awake in vain" (Ps 126:1). Elder Paisios of Mount Athos likened asceticism to the process of removing rust from a cable so that the "divine current" can flow freely. Ultimately, it is a response of love. "We love Him because He first loved us" (1 Jn 4:19). When understood as a response of love, asceticism encompasses more than just the external acts of offering up prayers, fasting, reading, vigils, and mortifying the body—it comprises the patient acceptance of the small annoyances, hardships, and sufferings of life, with humility and gratitude.

PSALM 109 (110)

"The Lord stands forth at Your right hand; He will crush kings in the day of His wrath"

One of the fathers in the Monastery of the Martyr St. Mina in Mariut recalled that in one of the liturgies at the monastery, after sprinkling the water and giving the holy bread, one of the fathers said to St. Pope Kyrillos VI, "There are only four people in the church." The Pope smiled and said to him, "Look at the southern section and you will see that the three pews at the back are full of the holy Anchorites."

Hearing those words, the monk's heart was heavy from his inability to see them. He thought to himself that the best way to have a chance of taking the blessing of seeing them was to fast and pray for three days and nights. He did so and on the third day, the Pope asked him to celebrate the Divine Liturgy at the northern Sanctuary.

When he started the Liturgy, the Pope left the Church and went to the church of Abba Samuel the Confessor. After praying the Thanksgiving Prayer, he could not say the Absolution as the Pope was present, since in the presence of the Patriarch, nobody else should pray it. So he stopped, waiting for the Pope to come. He waited a long while, then a luminous person appeared to him and told him to pray the Absolution. The monk went to the Sanctuary door and when he started saying the Absolution he saw a multitude entering the church through the southern door and bowing in reverence. They were not ordinary people but luminous figures. They remained until he finished the Absolution and then he could not see them; they disappeared in a flash. However, he enjoyed seeing them for a brief period.

Afterwards, the Pope came. There was a meaningful smile on his face. He did not ask him why the monk prayed the Absolution; from the way things went, it was obvious that he knew what was happening. After the Liturgy the monk said to him, "Your Holiness, I have seen great things today! I have seen the Anchorite Fathers." He said, "My son, those who are with us are greater than those who are against us."

On Mysticism

The word "mysticism" in modern usage is often conflated with various esoteric or obscure forms of knowledge. In his letters, St. Paul often repudiated the esoteric knowledge of the gnostics, declaring the true knowledge of the Gospel, the Mystery of Christ made known to him by revelation (Eph 3:3). In the spiritual life, mysticism is simply the divine activity taking place in the soul. It is the hidden presence of the Holy Spirit, through the Mysteries (Sacraments) and our devotional life, that often escapes the senses or observation. It has nothing to do with any external manifestation or psychological effect.

"The Kingdom of Heaven is like yeast that a woman took and mixed with three measures of flour until it was completely leavened" (Mt 13:31). The yeast is taken from a small pinch of dough and mixed with a batch of flour, yet over time it works through all the flour and produces dough that can be baked into bread. The leaven is the Divine life working in us, the kingdom within. God is the Mover and our work is not to resist - "Do not quench the Spirit" (1 Th 5:19).

Whereas asceticism relates more to exercise of the human will under the influence of grace, the mystical life is the initiative of the Holy Spirit working in the soul. The mystical life, then, is not something "extraordinary" in the sense of the charismatic gifts of the Holy Spirit (healings, prophecies, tongues, etc.) but the normal work of the Holy Spirit through the Church, taking place quietly and subtly in the souls of the believers. That does not mean that the benefit each person receives is the same, turning our receptivity into something passive. But just as asceticism depends on its support by grace, so the impact of the mystical work of the Holy Spirit depends on our readiness, preparedness, and cultivation. Mysticism and asceticism are inseparable.

PSALM 110 (111)

"I will give thanks to the Lord with all my heart"

A young woman asked her neighbor if she could accompany her to see St. Pope Kyrillos VI after hearing so much about him. She did not say anything about why she wanted to see him. On the way, the young woman asked about the proper protocol in greeting and addressing the Pope since it was her first time meeting a Christian clergyman, let alone someone as important as the Patriarch. She was told how to bow before him, kiss his hand, etc.

When they arrived at the Patriarchate and came into the presence of the Saint, he looked at the young woman and said, "Are you here under the protection of your neighbor?" She said, "No, Your Holiness, we all are under the protection of the Lord Jesus and Your Holiness." Then the girl approached him, bowed and kissed his hand but he immediately addressed her by her name and said, "He (the neighbor) gave you a lesson on protocol on your way here!" The girl was stunned. She had never met the Pope before, yet he knew her name and what had happened between them on the way.

The Pope did not give her a chance to speak about what was on her mind but started to talk with her about her problem and gave her the solution. It was a dilemma regarding her future and marriage. He said to her, "Tell your mother not to reject the one who proposes next. She should not be the one who makes this decision, as he is proposing to you, not to her!"

The girl was shocked. Here was her problem, fully exposed and disclosed to a man whom she never met, but clearly a true man of God!

It seems the girl's mother had rejected many young men who had asked the girl's hand in marriage. But the young man who was to propose next was truly fortunate. He married the girl as was revealed by the Saint, the one to whom the Lord had revealed the matter clearly.

On Newness in Life

"Vanity of vanities, all is vanity," says the Preacher in the Book of Ecclesiastes. The book might appear to some as the most pessimistic book in the Bible. The first eleven verses of the book are not very hopeful, "That which has been is what will be, that which is done is what will be done, and there is nothing new under the sun" (Ec 1:9). King Solomon cycles through a series of topics from toil, injustices, political corruption, dissatisfaction with possessions, and finally death, concluding that in all these there is no happiness, contentment, purpose, or satisfaction in life. Eventually, Solomon comes to the point of it all - this is what life looks like without God.

"Let us hear the conclusion of the whole matter: Fear God and keep His commandments, for this is man's all. For God will bring every work into judgment, including every secret thing, whether good or evil" (Ec 12:13, 14). In other words, there is no meaning in life unless we know God, love God and serve God. "See I am making all things new" (Re 21:5). The Resurrection of Christ and the gift of the Holy Spirit were pivotal realities in the lives of the Apostles. Their lives were completely transformed; their fears and confusion turned to excitement, joyful anticipation, and spiritual vigor. Do we view our faith as a series of religious rituals, and church as just one more thing in our busy lives? Or one of anticipation and hope?

This is the attitude of the saints. They never had the attitude of "it's just the same old!" They are always anticipating, hopeful, joyful, and waiting to be surprised by Christ! On the outside, it seems nothing changes in my life: same work, same family challenges, same social life, same daily routine...what is new? What is new is our "inward man." "Therefore we do not lose heart. Even though our outer self is continuing to decay, our inner self is being renewed day by day" (2 Co 4:16).

Through our union with Christ, we can discover a new attitude toward all that is happening in our life. Our continual "yes" to God in every circumstance of our life, even in the negative elements of our lives, will transform us and those around us.

PSALM 111 (112)

"He shines as a light for the upright in the darkness"

In 1966, a man faced a very serious problem and was advised by a friend to go and meet St. Pope Kyrillos VI. They were told that His Holiness was at St. Mina's Monastery in Mariut. They reached Mariut but were still 40 kilometers away when it was already getting dark. Still determined to go, bedouins who overheard them talking said they knew the way. They took him in the car but ended up in the vast desert with no track to follow. A boy of about nine years of age signaled for them to stop. He told them that he knew the way and with his help they were able to reach the monastery. The man went inside and left the two guides outside.

The Saint had just gone to his cell but the man asked to see him. The Pope listened to him, all the while smiling at him while the man spoke and looking at him as if he was a book the Pope was reading. The Saint told him regarding his problem that the path was not going to be easy and that he would face many difficulties. But he comforted the man by saying that at the end nothing would happen to him and that he would be saved from his dilemma. The Saint dismissed him saying, "God is with you."

It was almost midnight, and when they were about to leave, the Pope called out to one of the monks saying, "Tell him!" The monk came to the man and said, "You have two guides with you, listen to the young one but be cautious of the old. If he says go left, refuse, no matter what!" He repeated these words more than once and said that God will protect them and that St. Mina's blessing will accompany them and guide them in the desert.

The young guide left when they reached the place where they picked him up. The older guide asked them to turn left and by that time they forgot what the monk had told them. They thought they were giving the man a ride to his home but found themselves in a very deserted area where he asked them to stop. Suddenly, they were surrounded by about 50 men who demanded money. They took five pounds and while waiting to get more change, they heard that three of the men were digging graves!

But St. Mina's blessing and the St. Pope Kyrillos' prayers protected them. They managed to escape slaughter by a miracle. It was through a divine power that the driver asked the man who was sitting in the front of the car to move aside and then they took off! They then remembered the warning given to them at the monastery. The main problem that was troubling the man ended peacefully as the Saint said and God's Name was glorified.

On Biblical Spirituality

The Bible is not written as a manual on the spiritual life. Rather, it is a history of what God has done in the lives of men and for humanity, which invites us, inspires us, and guides us on a spiritual journey. What is clear throughout the Bible is that God initiates everything. It is He Who establishes and guarantees an everlasting covenant with mankind. "I will be your God and you shall be My people" (Je 7:23). And equally, "I will be a Father to him, and he shall be a son to Me" (2 Sa 7:14). God is Emmanuel: "God with us." He is not only active in history but in every detail of my life.

God approaches man, revealing to man his great destiny, and responding to man's innate desire to experience divine life. Man, by his free will offers himself to God, allowing God to fulfill His will in him and in the world. Within this framework, we can understand and appreciate the urgency of the Bible's message. "The kingdom of God is at hand. Repent, and believe in the gospel" (Mk 1:15). It is a matter of life and death. Likewise, the Bible demands a certain radicality. "Therefore you shall be perfect, just as your Father in heaven is perfect" (Mt 5:48). Superficiality must be rejected.

The Bible testifies to God's everlasting faithfulness, inspiring man's confidence and trust in God. "If we are faithless, he remains faithful; he cannot deny Himself" (2 Ti 2:13). His faithfulness overcomes humanity's wickedness, the destructive nature of sin, and affirms over and over again a spirituality of hope and joy.

The spirituality of the Bible is both personal and communal, vertical, and horizontal. "I am the vine, you are the branches" (Jn 15:5). "If someone says, 'I love God,' and hates his brother, he is a liar; for he who does not love his brother whom he has seen, how can he love God whom he has not seen?" (1 Jn 4:20).

PSALM 112 (113)

"Who dwells in the high places, and looks upon the low things"

St. Pope Kyrillos VI once met an elderly gentleman accompanied by a young lady who was his relative. Though he had never met them before, as soon as His Holiness saw this elderly gentleman, he stood up and welcomed him by his name saying, "Uncle Botros, please pray and call upon the Lord for me!"

The elderly gentleman was overwhelmed by the Pope's clairvoyance and the fact that in such humility he stood to welcome him. He was surprised that the saintly Pope was imploring him, a layman, to pray for him. In fact, this gentleman was living a holy celibate life and spending all his money on his nephews and others.

The Saint also gave joy and consolation to this self-sacrificing gentleman by turning to his relative, the young lady that accompanied him, and said, "May the Lord give you a son and name him Botros [after the elderly man]." The man was filled with great joy and left the Pope very happy. Surprisingly, the young lady was already at the very beginning of her pregnancy.

On God's Condescension

The descent and condescension of God, Who takes to Himself our human nature and dwells amongst us, has the principal aim of persuading us of His consummate love. "Having loved His own who were in the world, He loved them to the end" (Jn 13:1). He chooses His own condescension in order to esteem and exalt. "He humbled Himself that He may lift us up. He hungered to satiate us, and thirsted to quench our thirst. And He ascended upon the Cross naked that He might clothe us with the garment of His righteousness" (*Fraction to the Son, Divine Liturgy of St. Basil*).

The condescension of God is a hiddenness and divestiture of His majesty, and self-evident Presence. St. Ephrem the Syrian reminds us that Jesus began in a manger and finished with a donkey! The hiddenness of God is a stumbling block for those who demand a sign (Mt 14:4), but a cause of consolation for those who know how to find

Him by faith. For God can conceal Himself behind human flesh, and the bread and wine, but His majesty is uncovered by faith. His voice in the silence; His light in the darkness; His consolation in the desolation; His mercy in the sin; His hope in despair; His joy in the weeping; His possession in the desire; His friendship in the loneliness; His fatherhood in the abandonment.

The condescension of God is simultaneously a judgment on the world. It is a judgment on our pride and hardened hearts. How will we stand before Him Who was scorned, humiliated, and stripped on our behalf when we are not willing to humble ourselves before Him and before our fellows? What justification shall we give when He Who exposes to us His wounds says, "Reach your finger here, and look at My hands; and reach your hand here, and put it into My side" (Jn 20:27). Even if we humble ourselves before God, we will not be justified. To resemble Jesus, we must also humble ourselves before those whom we deem to be lesser, inferior, and weaker to ourselves. A spirituality of condescension means I am pleased to lift up my neighbor above myself, to give him the first place and retain for myself the last place.

PSALM 114 (116)

"I was seized by distress and sorrow. O Lord deliver my soul"

On March 1, 2006, a mother passed by the church daycare to pick up her two-and-half-year-old son after work. However, she did not find him. Filled with fear, she rushed inside the church and with many tears she implored St. Pope Kyrillos VI through his icon, saying, "Your Holiness, you bring back my child, you look for him!"

She left the church and, with the director from the daycare, they searched everywhere for more than an hour. All the while, she was imploring St. Pope Kyrillos VI to save her from catastrophe. Suddenly, she had the thought to go home, thinking he might be there. This would have been nearly impossible, and dangerous, since her son was so young. The distance from the church and her home would take about fifteen minutes.

To her great surprise, she found him at home! When she asked him what happened, he said, "I heard you calling me and when I came out of the church, I did not find you. As I was looking for you, I saw Abouna [Father] - and he pointed to the picture of St. Pope Kyrillos VI - who held my hand and I walked with him all the way home." The mother started crying and praising the Lord!

On Crucifying the Mind

St. Paul, writing to the Galatians, admonished the Christian community to categorically transition from living according to the law to living by grace, from the flesh to the Spirit. "And those who belong to Christ have crucified the flesh with its passions and desires. If we live by the Spirit, let us also be guided by the Spirit" (Ga 5:24-25). The Cross of Christ initiated an unraveling of human logic and wisdom. That is why those who insist to remain living "according to the flesh" will always find the Cross "a stumbling block...and...foolishness" (1 Co 1:23).

How we need to continually crucify our minds! All our ideas, thoughts, and judgments need to be placed at the foot of the Cross, buried in the tomb, and raised and transfigured by the Spirit of God. How many have become lukewarm, live sorrowfully, or even abandoned their faith and rejected God, because they insisted on reconciling the flesh with the Spirit, man's ways with God's ways? "'For My thoughts are not your thoughts, nor are your ways My ways,' says the LORD. 'For as the heavens are higher than the earth, so are My ways higher than your ways, and My thoughts than your thoughts'" (Is 55:8, 9).

The Mother of God is the greatest example of one who completely submitted her thoughts, plans, obedience, and her complete will to God. One example from the Scriptures illustrates this beautifully. In the order of greatness St. Mary, the Mother of God, is above St. Joseph, the martyrs, the angels and archangels, and all the heavenly hosts. And yet, when God gradually unfolds His plan in the world, we find that the angel of the Lord appears to St. Joseph three times (Mt 2:13, 19, 22) with the details of the flight to Egypt and their return. St. Mary obeys St. Joseph perfectly; she does not raise any objections or complaints. She does not ask why the angel had not appeared to her. After all, it was the angel that appeared to her to announce the birth of Christ. In her perfect love, trust, and obedience to God, she does not live according to the flesh, or human logic. She has put on the mind of Christ. "For 'who has known the mind of the Lord that he may instruct Him?' But we have the mind of Christ" (1 Co 2:16).

PSALM 115 (116)

"I will offer You a sacrifice of thanksgiving and call on the Name of the Lord"

The police superintendent from a nearby governorate came to visit the Monastery of the Great Martyr St. Mina at Mariut during the early stages of construction. When he shook hands with St. Pope Kyrillos VI, the Pope noticed that he moved his arm with difficulty, so he asked him, "What is wrong, my son?" The superintendent answered, "I have severe rheumatism. Medication has been useless and the physicians can't seem to do anything."

The Saint's heart was touched and he had compassion for the man. The Pope then made the sign of the Cross on the man's arm and said, "It is all gone, now you are fine." In an instant, the man's arm became well and he was able to move it freely. There was no trace of illness left. He was full of joy and gave thanks to the Pope who relieved him from his pain.

A few days later, the superintendent came with some other men and planted pear trees all around the land of the monastery. He did that in great gratitude to the Lord Who granted him recovery at the hands of this great saint.

On Dissatisfied Love

A sign of great holiness among the saints is dissatisfied love. Overwhelmed by God's love and goodness, they feel great pain in their hearts for not responding proportionately. One's prayer becomes increasingly about the grace to love more: "Lord, I want to love You as You ought to be loved!" Loving God in measure becomes an obsession and the heart becomes unsettled with a holy restlessness.

It is a share in St. Peter's tremendous grief as the words of the Lord incessantly ring in the heart, "Do you love me?" (Jn 21:17). That simple question is enough to open the flood gates of remorseful tears. But these tears are mixed with joy and hope because the foundation of these tears is love and in that love, God consoles us. St. John Climacus calls it "joyful sadness."

Dissatisfied love has many attributes; if we are genuinely dissatisfied with our love for God, we will likewise be dissatisfied with our love for our neighbor and our enemy. We will see everyone else as better than ourselves. When St. Antony the Great was told by the Lord that he had not yet reached the level of sanctity as a tanner living in the world, St. Antony traveled to Alexandria anxious to discover his secret. The mystery of his sanctity was not some extreme ascetic feats, nor was it his lofty prayer life. It was that he did not see anything good in his works, and that he believed and said in his heart every day that everyone in the town would go to the Kingdom of God except him.

One of the fathers said that the higher a tree wishes to ascend, the lower into the earth it penetrates its roots. The greater the knowledge of our own misery and nothingness, the more God's grace will raise us into a beautiful temple for His dwelling. A mother is pleased with observing her child who wants to do more to please her, all the while assuring her child that she unconditionally loves them as they are.

THE ELEVENTH HOUR

PSALM 116 (117)

"His mercy has been established upon us, and the faithfulness of the Lord will endure forever"

A certain man, well-known to St. Pope Kyrillos VI, used to pass by the cathedral of St. Mark every morning to take the blessing of the Pope on his way to work. On one occasion, the Saint looked at him, smiled and said to him, "Wait, I want you for something." The man waited five minutes, then another five minutes passed as he anxiously looked at his watch because he had to go to work.

The Pope remained greeting and blessing a long line of people. The man whispered in the ear of someone standing next to him, "I have to go to work." But the Saint looked at him, and again, said "Wait." Finally, after twenty minutes the Pope looked at him and said, "Ok, my son, thank God. Go to work safely."

The man was very surprised and frustrated thinking, "Why all this delay? And at the end, simply 'Go to work'?" So, he hurried to his work in the downtown area, which was about five minutes away. When he arrived, he found the employees standing in the street saying to him, "You are so fortunate! You have never been late except for today and it was to your advantage. The ceiling inside the office collapsed just over your desk ten minutes ago! If you were here, you would have died!"

The man closed his eyes and thought, "That's why the Saint said, 'Thank God. Go to work safely.'...He saw what was going to happen and prevented me from leaving."

On Doubts

It is natural for our intellect to doubt what it neither sees nor understands. Sometimes doubt is caused by ignorance which we have to remedy through further instruction or knowledge. But other times, doubt is a temptation not unlike any other temptation we face. We are not immune from any form of temptation, but in all cases we overcome temptation by an act of the will. "Without having seen Him (i.e., Christ), you love Him; though you do not now see Him, you believe in Him and rejoice with joy unutterable and full of glory" (1 Pe 1:8).

Doubt is to faith what fear is to courage. A courageous person is not one who does not experience fear, but one who acts courageously in the face of fear. Similarly, what is required in times of doubt is the will to act faithfully. That means to live and act as one who has faith, persisting in our prayers, worship, spiritual reading, and daily acts of entrusting ourselves to God until the temptation passes. Through these trials of doubts, our faith is strengthened and purified. There can be no genuine faith without doubt.

What is required of us is sincerity. St. Thomas was not incredulous. He was honest and sincere. Similarly, in the Gospel, Jesus said to a man whose son had an unclean spirit, "If you can believe, all things are possible to him who believes." Immediately the father of the child cried out and said with tears, "Lord, I believe; help my unbelief!" (Mk 9:24). Nor was St. Thomas the only disciple who doubted. Curiously, in his Gospel account, St. Matthew says that the eleven disciples went to Galilee to the mountain which Jesus had directed them. There, "When they saw Him, they worshiped Him; but some doubted" (Mt 28:17).

Faith can never be reduced to a feeling; our feelings will never provide any stability for a virtue to flourish. Faith requires a choice to believe, always involving a risk and a commitment. "Blessed are those who have not seen and have believed" (Jn 20:29).

PSALM 117 (118)

"In my distress I called out to the Lord; and He answered by setting me free"

A certain man, through his friend, came to know St. Pope Kyrillos VI when he was still Fr. Mina the Solitary. He was greatly impressed by the height of the Saint's spirituality.

After his friend's death, he continued visiting Fr. Mina with his friend's wife until she became ill and couldn't visit him anymore.

Fr. Mina asked the man where she was, and when he informed the Saint about her illness, he gave the man a piece of cotton with holy oil with which to anoint her. He doubted the effectiveness of this gesture, but he said nothing.

On another visit, Fr. Mina again asked him about his friend's wife and he told him she was still ill and in pain. He quietly said that he would visit her. Because she lived in an area of great poverty, he told him that he would bring him a taxi. Fr. Mina smiled and told him not to worry and that he would go by other means. He wondered how he would go since he did not even have her address.

When the man went to see the lady, he hesitated to tell her about what Fr. Mina said, because he doubted the Saint would actually go. He was surprised, however, to find her in perfect health. She informed him that Fr. Mina had come to her while she was awake and he was accompanied by a young man with long hair who treated her like a doctor and prayed over her until she felt well. Then, they left.

On Lukewarmness

One of the best descriptions of lukewarmness in the spiritual life is that of a "soul tired of love." We can think of what happens in a marriage when one or both spouses are "tired" of the effort and sacrifice that love demands. How quickly things unravel. First, small things, then bigger ones. Lukewarmness is a spiritual sickness that attacks both the intellect and the will, undermining the strength to carry out one's duties toward love. It is a loss of enthusiasm and gratitude, and leads to discouragement and timidity.

Spiritual hunger is a sign of a healthy and active spirit. Lukewarmness is a loss of hunger for God, a lack of desire to seek Him. It is a soul that has become insensible. But we must not confuse lukewarmness with aridity or dryness. Aridity is an experience more at the level of the senses or emotions, and not the will, which is still firmly set on God and fulfilling His commandments. In times of dryness, we might find it difficult to pray, but our devotion to God has not wavered. Just as in a healthy marriage, there are times of passion but also times of dry sacrifice. Nonetheless, commitment and fidelity are unwavering.

A warning sign that lukewarmness is setting in is when we give little importance to the small acts of piety and the struggle toward virtue. The more we ignore them, the more we will end up paying no attention to the big things. We must remain on guard to avoid suffering from what C.S. Lewis calls "the horror of the same old thing." Jesus has no use for half-hearted disciples. "No one who puts his hand to the plow and then looks back is fit for the Kingdom of God" (Lk 9:61)

There will always be ups and downs in the spiritual life. We must always be ready to begin again. Spiritual struggle demands a love that is watchful. Lukewarmness is a lack of interest and care in seeking God, doing His will and fulfilling our obligations toward Him.

PSALM 119 (120)

"Deliver me, O Lord, from lying lips and from deceitful tongues"

A certain man's wife was unjustly transferred from her school which caused her great suffering because of the long commute. They attempted to appeal the decision at the Ministry of Education. Before going, they decided to first visit St. Pope Kyrillos VI.

When they arrived they were told they could not see him because it was in the middle of the ordination of two new bishops. At the Ministry of Education, they were unable to achieve anything and there seemed to be no sign of hope. They returned to the Patriarchate and sat in the upstairs reception room. One of the fathers told them that His Holiness was resting because he had spent the whole night in prayers, followed by the ordination of the new bishops which finished around 2:00 p.m. It was about 2:20 p.m. and it was impossible to disturb His Holiness after such a brief rest.

Of course, they did not insist on seeing His Holiness after what they heard about his long night and morning. They were offered a drink in celebration of the new bishops and then were preparing to leave. They took one step toward the door to leave when the side door of the reception room opened and they saw His Holiness standing there with a very dignified appearance. He turned to them and said, "I came out especially for you so you would not be upset!" So the husband asked him, "Did anyone tell Your Holiness that we were upset?" He answered, "Yes, the Honest and Loyal One told me!" The man could not understand what His Holiness meant until he said to his wife, "You will return to your school again and God will spoil the plans of those who caused your transfer. Go in peace, the peace of the Lord be with you!"

They were surprised to hear these words as they did not mention anything to anyone about the transfer. They realized then that it was the Holy Spirit Who revealed this to him. They left full of joy after a miserable day. A few days later, they received a letter from the Ministry of Education cancelling the transfer and the wife returned to her original school. It seems as though the Saint was reading everything from an open book.

On Spiritual Vulnerability with God

The word vulnerable comes from the Latin *vulnus,* which means "wound". Vulnerability is "wound-ability". It is the possibility and openness to being wounded or hurt. Thus, it also implies transparency. Through the Incarnation, God has accepted to enter the experience of vulnerability. The helplessness of an infant, poverty, threats, and violence are just some of the vulnerable areas that, often painfully and sorrowfully, touched Christ's life.

To love is to suffer. Since Jesus loved the most, He suffered the most. The journey toward a deeper interior spiritual life is an odyssey of vulnerability because it is a journey into greater and more intimate love. Intimacy and vulnerability go hand in hand. Spouses journey together on the way of vulnerability.

Little children, through their vulnerability, best express this wisdom of God. The virtue of simplicity hinges on a certain defenselessness before God which requires childlike trust. The famous Western saint, Therese of Lisieux, insisted that prayer must embrace a level of familiarity with God as with a friend. That includes, she said, sharing with Him all that we carry in our hearts from the events of the day, the behavior of others, and our reactions and feelings. She was questioned why we should do this since God already knows all these things. Her response was that in order to give and to receive love, He descends to us, dealing with us as if He has forgotten that He knows everything, so that He might hear an intimate word from our hearts.

We see in the Gospel how much our Lord appreciated and rewarded the vulnerability of others. Zacchaeus, the Sinful Woman, blind Bartimaeus, and so many of the nameless sick and demon-possessed all manifested a level of vulnerability which attracted Christ to their aid and, often, to friendship. We can begin to practice vulnerability with God first in our prayer life. Speaking to Him honestly about our sins, guilt, and shame, and learning to accept the free gift of God's tender mercy. Without such vulnerability before God, we will never experience Christ's tremendous healing power.

PSALM 120 (121)

"My help comes from the Lord, the Maker of heaven and earth"

In 1969, a mother gave birth to a baby girl whose health began to deteriorate quickly after birth. The physicians were unable to help and they all believed the baby had only a few hours to live.

She decided to visit St. Mark's Cathedral to take the blessing of St. Pope Kyrillos VI, taking along her neighbor. Her neighbor, who was not a Christian, would hemorrhage and miscarry every time she became pregnant. Once they arrived, the lady asked her non-Christian neighbor to wait in the hallway while she met with St. Pope Kyrillos. She went in with her newborn baby and asked the Saint to pray for her. He laid his blessed hand on the baby's head and said a long prayer. Afterwards, he turned to the mother and said, "Don't worry about your baby. She will grow up and get married."

To her great surprise, he also said, "Now go and tell the lady that came with you to come in." She had not mentioned anything about her neighbor and was surprised that he knew she was there. The lady rushed out to get her neighbor and St. Pope Kyrillos prayed for her also. Soon, her neighbor became pregnant and everything this time went smoothly. As the Saint said, the baby girl grew up and got married and had two children of her own.

On the Hidden Life

When our Lord healed the paralytic (Lk 15:17-26), He revealed that in the domain of the Spirit, the things which are hidden are greater than the things which are uncovered. "Which is easier, to say, 'Your sins are forgiven you,' or to say, 'Rise up and walk'?" Certainly, the forgiveness of sins which Our Savior extends is greater than any physical healing. For the former leads to eternal life, while physical health is at best enjoyed momentarily on earth. Everything in the apostolic life and in our external good deeds flows from our interior life, hidden from the world and known only to God. "For you died, and your life is hidden with Christ in God" (Col 3:3).

The Incarnation is an expression of God's hiddenness in Jesus. His "form," St. Paul tells us, was that of a slave (Php 2:7) not the Lord of Glory. But even if the disciples were granted a glimpse beyond this concealment in the event of the Transfiguration, there is yet another level of hiddenness in Jesus: His interior life within the Holy Trinity. We are called to imitate Christ in His hiddenness. First, this consists in hiding ourselves from the eyes of others, and even ourselves, dying to worldly glory and honor. And secondly, a deep interior life centered on intimacy with God.

"Do not let your adornment be merely outward–arranging the hair, wearing gold, or putting on fine apparel–rather let it be the hidden person of the heart, with the incorruptible beauty of a gentle and quiet spirit, which is very precious in the sight of God" (1 Pe 3:3-4). The "adornment" St. Peter refers to need not only refer to physical beautification, but also the adornment of outward virtue and talents. Hiddenness is a proof of genuineness, and God only approves of what is genuine in us. If, then, we truly desire the hidden life, we must "shut the door," and seek our "Father who is in the secret place" (Mt 6:6).

PSALM 121 (122)

"I rejoiced when they said to me, 'Let us go to the house of the Lord'"

A certain monk was in charge of lighting the lamps in front of the saints' icons in the Church of St. Mina in Old Cairo. He used to sleep in the baptistry room. Late one night, he saw a venerable old man dressed in priestly vestments with light emanating from him. His face was like that of an angel, and he was holding a censer. He came closer to the monk and the monk became frightened. He was surprised to find the whole church lit. He asked, "Who lit the lamps?"

Then, he found himself in the presence of luminous people. They motioned to him to keep silent and great fear came upon him. The elder priest approached him and held him to get up. The monk said fearfully, "Leave me." He replied, "I want you." These words took away his fear and he gained some courage. He said to the monk, "Come, come. You ate at 11:00 p.m. If you had not eaten, I would have given you Holy Communion." The monk asked, "How did you know?" He answered, "God," and pointed his finger up to heaven.

The monk walked to the church and found it filled with the holy Anchorites, and Fr. Mina the Solitary (St. Pope Kyrillos VI) was among them. They were all dressed in white and their appearance was venerable like the angels. Their voices were very beautiful. He never heard such beautiful voices in his life and they were praying with awe and reverence.

He approached each one of the Anchorites to take their blessings and they were looking at him and smiling. Then, he sat among them until the end of the Divine Liturgy until the priest who was serving said, "Glory to God in the Highest...," and he sprinkled the water, then they left.

How they left! A beautiful and amazing thing happened! This whole gathering of saints turned into white doves, hovering up high then flying out from the church dome. He heard the rustling of their wings while they were flying leaving the church. All this took approximately an hour and a half, which he spent in Paradise through the blessing of his father and teacher, Fr. Mina the Solitary.

Fr. Mina the Solitary, as usual, did not talk to the monk about anything, but he knew what happened, since he asked him the next day not to sleep in the baptistry again. When the monk asked about the reason, he said to him that he disturbed the Anchorites the night before. And indeed, he did not sleep there again. He started sleeping in the room where the holy bread was made but he was very sad. After a week, one of the Anchorites came to him and told him not to be sad, and that he should obey his father because obedience is a wonderful thing. He stressed that he should be obedient to him with all his heart and he blessed him and left.

On the Nature of Spiritual Consolations and Desolations

At the level of our emotions, senses, and psychological experiences, the spiritual life is a constant series of peaks and valleys. At times we feel great joy in our spiritual journey and at times that joy is depressed; encouraging and discouraging moods, uplifting experiences and dry displeasing periods. These fluctuations can be frustrating and discouraging. We assume we are doing something wrong, and that God is withholding His grace from us because of His displeasure. In spiritual theology, the terms "consolation" and "desolation" are often used to describe these oscillations in our relationship with God. Understanding what they are–and what they are not–and learning from the saints on how to respond to them, is one of the most vital concerns in an authentic, spiritual life.

""For My thoughts are not your thoughts, nor are your ways My ways," says the Lord" (Is 55:8). Mistakenly, we assume that spiritual life should always tend upward, never going backward, that our weaknesses are removed by our desire and ascetic struggles, and that spiritual life should be an ever increasing experience of fervor and zeal. But these are not God's ways of leading us to perfection. Moving forward often means being thrown back. Purification and humility come with temptations and falls; trust and reliance come by finding our human efforts faltering again and again. We need to be at peace with these experiences, trusting that "God's ways are not our ways" and discern how to respond to them.

The first distinction to be made is identifying if a consolation or desolation is "spiritual" or "non-spiritual". Listening to my favorite song on my drive to work may put me in a good mood, consoling as it may be, but that is not a spiritual consolation. Getting a paper cut can be frustrating, but that is not a spiritual desolation. The key is whether the consolation or desolation impacts my faith, hope, and love for God and my ability to follow His will. Examples of spiritual consolations include spiritual attractions, feelings or experiences of greater love for God and eternal life, ease, and delight in prayer, tears that accompany contrition, and a strong desire to surrender one's life to God. Examples of spiritual desolations include discouragement in spiritual life, doubts about God, feelings of abandonment by God, aridity in prayer, and a greater attraction to sin and earthly things.

PSALM 122 (123)

"Unto You I have lifted up my eyes, O You who dwell in heaven"

A certain lady's son was living abroad and at one point the family stopped receiving any correspondence from him. They started to become anxious and afraid. They had a large icon of St. George, and in the corner of its frame was a small picture of St. Pope Kyrillos VI.

She had never seen St. Pope Kyrillos VI when he was alive and had not heard anything about his miracles up to that point. However, something inside her prompted her to look deeply at his picture and speak to him. She said, "O, Pope Kyrillos! I never saw you when you were in our world, but now that you have reposed I cry out to you to pray for us! Plead with our Lady that I might receive a letter to calm my anxious heart."

After about half an hour, the doorbell rang. There was a young man holding a letter. He said, "I was abroad with your son and he gave me this letter about a month ago and I completely forgot about it. I am really sorry. I just remembered it a few minutes before I came."

The time from when she spoke to the Saint through his picture until the time she received the letter was about the same amount of time it takes to get from where he was to her house.

On the Purpose and Response to Spiritual Consolations and Desolations

Consolations are not necessary for spiritual growth. That might sound strange, but we must recall that consolations and desolations deal with our feelings, emotions, and experiences. They tend to be at the level of the senses and psyche. In fact, we grow more spiritually in the absence of consolations if our will is inclined toward God and the virtues. For example, it is clearly more difficult, more virtuous, and therefore more meritorious, to be patient with an annoying person when I am sick or suffering, than when I am in a great and happy mood. Likewise, it is more virtuous to do God's will, to pray, and to serve, when I do not have the emotional support of consolations.

Desolations in fact have many benefits in the spiritual life. They act as "wake-up" calls, leading us to repentance and greater conversion. Through desolations we gain self-knowledge. Desolations purify us of self-love and lead us to the blessedness of spiritual poverty (Mt 5:3), teach us patient endurance (Lk 21:19), and refine our love by seeking the pleasure of the other above my own pleasure. "It is more blessed to give than to receive" (Ac 20:35).

So we should accept consolations as a "treat" from God with gratitude from which we try to procure new ardor toward Him. In times of consolation, we meditate on God's faithfulness which supports and encourages us to continue on our way, entrusting Him with our spiritual journey. This is the time to prepare for the inevitable ensuing period of desolation, acknowledging its benefits, and committing ourselves by God's grace to resist discouragement. In times of desolation, we should think from God's perspective, Who desires to thrust my spiritual life forward by affording me the possibility of demonstrating my love, and by acting by my will, even if unsupported by my emotions and senses. And finally, I can rest in God's arms knowing that He will soon console me at the time He knows best.

PSALM 123 (124)

"If the Lord had not been on our side when our enemies attacked us, then they would have swallowed us up alive"

In 1968, the Patriarchate was going through a tough financial crisis and the President of the country graciously offered a ten thousand pound grant. However, the Ministry of Agricultural Development surprised the Patriarch with a request for payment of 150,000 pounds.

The Ministry had recently taken over land where St. Antony's Monastery was built. The Ministry claimed that the Patriarchate owed the price of the land of St. Antony's Monastery, in addition to the rent and interest on the land of the El-Muharraq Monastery, a sum that came to an extra 150,000 pounds. It was a ludicrous and unjust claim.

The lawyer brought this disturbing news to St. Pope Kyrillos VI. The Saint smiled and said, "Leave the papers for three days and the Lord will take care of the situation."

He celebrated three consecutive Liturgies each day ending at sunset after fasting all day. After the Divine Liturgy on the third day, the Saint, full of joy, met the attorney and told him, "O son, the government is the one who owes us money." Surprised, the attorney asked how this could possibly be. His Holiness said to him, "Review closely the President's decree and see what it says: 'The government will compensate the owners for any land it takes over.' They took the land at St. Antony's, therefore they owe us its price. But they did not proceed to take the land at El-Muharraq, therefore we owe them nothing." When the calculations were made, it was found that the government owed the Patriarchate 250,000 pounds.

When the Saint was asked about how he knew these details while the file for the case was in the attorney's office, he responded, "St. Mina told me!" St. Mina revealed the truth of the matter to St. Pope Kyrillos VI after fasting and praying for three days.

On Joy

We often confuse pleasure, happiness, and joy. Though in modern secular usage these words might be used synonymously, in the spiritual life a clear distinction will be valuable. Pleasure is usually associated with the body and the senses. Enjoying a delicious meal, the scent of an elegant perfume, and watching a beautiful sunset are examples of pleasures. Happiness is the satisfaction of my mind, emotions, feelings and perceptions of things "happening" around me. But authentic joy, understood properly, is the possession of a spiritual good and the fruit of God's infinite, divine love. That's why St. Paul can boldly insist, "Rejoice in the Lord always. Again I will say, rejoice!" (Php 4:4). Though we might not always be capable of being happy, and certainly we can not always be in a state of pleasure, we do have the possibility of always experiencing joy.

Joy is divine love brought near, much like a mother's love for her children who all live in different places is turned into joy when they all gather around her for the holidays. But for joy to be genuine, must it be felt? It is possible that genuine joy also produces happiness and pleasure which are felt at some level in the senses and emotions. But joy can never be reduced to the level of feelings and emotions. That is why in the lives of the saints, the martyrs could experience joy in their sufferings, the prisoners in their exile, and the sick in their afflictions. Certainly none of these experiences are happy or pleasurable ones. "I tell you the truth, you will weep and mourn while the world rejoices. You will grieve, but your grief will turn to joy" (Jn 16:20). Jesus' suffering was truly agonizing and yet joyful because of His love for us.

Joy is also the fruit of hope. The Resurrection is the fulfillment of our joy. We know how the story ends! Our inheritance is eternal life with the Trinity, the angels and the saints. Triumph is assured through hope. "Now hope does not disappoint, because the love of God has been poured out in our hearts by the Holy Spirit Who was given to us" (Ro 5:5). If our sorrows and pains suffocate our joy, then it means we have ceased hoping. Joy is our inheritance but also our obligation. We do not receive it passively, but we work hard every day to acquire and maintain it. It is no less an ascetic effort than prayer, fasting, and vigils.

PSALM 124 (125)

"Do good, O Lord, to those who are good, to those that are upright of heart"

During the war of June 1967, one man decided to move his family from Suez to Beni-Suef to keep them safe while he stayed in Suez for work. He would visit his family once or twice a month whenever possible. On the way, he would go to Saint Mark's Cathedral in Cairo, to take the blessing of St. Pope Kyrillos VI.

On one of those visits, the Saint was late in coming out of his room to bless those gathered in the reception area. While waiting, the man became steadily anxious that he would miss his train. However, he insisted on taking the blessing from the Saint and decided to wait until the last possible moment. As the departure time for the train drew very near, he decided to leave the waiting room. Right then, the Saint came out of his room to bless those present. The man decided to stay and take his blessing even if it meant missing the train.

When it was his turn to receive the blessing, he kissed the hand of the Pope. After he prayed for him, His Holiness said to him, "Walk slowly and don't worry. The train will wait for you, and will not move until you get on it." He repeated those same words several times.

The man marveled at the Saint's words as he walked slowly to the train station. He kept thinking about what happened and asked himself: "How did the Pope know that I was traveling? How did he know that I was already late for the train? His Holiness does not know about the train, nor does he even know me personally!"

As he arrived at the station, he was sure that the train had left, since it was already very late. He went to the ticket counter to get a ticket for the next train while holding the old ticket in his hand. The ticket attendant asked him what ticket he was holding in his hand. He answered him that it was for the 4:00p.m. train which certainly must have already left by now. To the man's surprise, the attendant said to him, "Who told you that it has already left? The train is still in the station. Hurry up and catch it!"

As soon as he got on the train, it started moving.

On Docility

Docility is the willingness to be taught and guided. The virtue of docility refers to our yielding to the influence of the Holy Spirit, the teachings of the Lord, the Church and our spiritual fathers. It is one of the striking contrasts between the disciples and the Pharisees. "But blessed are your eyes for they see, and your ears for they hear...Therefore hear the parable" (Mt 13:16-18). Docility is a reminder that so much of the spiritual life is not about what we do for God but letting God attract us, instruct us and guide us. What makes the disciples' eyes and ears "blessed" is that they are in a state of humble receptivity. The Pharisees, however, display a cold rigidity which blinds them. Jesus tells them, "but since you claim, 'we see,' your guilt remains" (Jn 9:41).

The spiritually mature person is always docile to the workings of God through a humble openness which accepts correction from others. One day, St. Pachomius the Great was visiting one of the monastic communities under his care and he sat down to weave some mats. A young boy visiting the monastery that day saw the saint doing his work and, not knowing that this was not only a revered elder but the father of the whole community, approached him saying, "Not so father! Do not turn the thread this way. Father Theodore showed us another style of weaving." St. Pachomius rose and said to the boy, "Yes, teach me this style!" After the boy taught him, the saint sat to work gladly.

Docility also means a willingness to abandon one's will swiftly and without calculation in order to fulfill God's will. Jesus had taken the disciples to a deserted place for some much-needed rest and fellowship (Mk 6:31-32). But immediately the crowds followed them. "And Jesus, when He came out, saw a great multitude and was moved with compassion for them, because they were like sheep not having a shepherd" (Mk 6:34). Jesus began to teach the people and the disciples were called out of their rest to serve the people. Docility makes it possible for us to accept with joy when our plans are disrupted in order to fulfill God's will. We learn the art of surrender and abandonment to God, attuned to the present moment.

PSALM 125 (126)

"The Lord has indeed done great deeds for us, and we are overflowing with joy"

A certain man took his friend who was facing a problem to visit Fr. Mina the Solitary (St. Pope Kyrillos VI) at the Church of St. Mina in Old Cairo to consult with him on the problem.

When they arrived, they saw a large number of people waiting to meet Fr. Mina who was sitting with one of his guests. The problem needed immediate attention and since they already waited for a long time, he approached the door of the room and noticed that Fr. Mina was speaking with a young officer who was sitting right beside him.

Fr. Mina kept smiling and they were speaking intimately as if they were very close friends. As one talked, the other smiled and listened as if they were discussing an important matter. He assumed that this officer was a friend of Fr. Mina's who had come to help him or a member of the congregation with a problem, so he withdrew quickly.

After some time, he went back to the door and the officer was still talking. Thirty minutes later, Fr. Mina opened the door and came out without the officer. The friend spoke to Fr. Mina about his problem while the man kept thinking about the officer.

Fr. Mina looked intently at him as if reading his thoughts. The man drew close to him and asked him, "My Father, we waited for such a long time and whenever I tried to come in, I saw an officer beside you and the two of you were talking."

The Saint replied, "An officer? An officer? Oh, my son, where is that officer that would be concerned with us?" But the man insisted that he saw him. Then Fr. Mina asked him, "Was he sitting on my left side or on my right side?" He answered, "He sat on your right hand."

He replied very simply and meekly, "Oh, my son, he is St. Mina!"

On Being a Sign of Contradiction

A strong fragrance for one person can be an ecstatic inebriation and for another the same fragrance can cause a violent, repugnant reaction. Christ's coming to our world caused division at His time and it continues. "Do not think that I came to bring peace on earth. I did not come to bring peace but a sword" (Mt 10:34). Jesus is a sign of contradiction, or opposition. This was a title bestowed on him prophetically by St. Simeon the Elder, "Behold, this Child is destined for the fall and for the rise of many in Israel, and for a sign that shall be contradicted" (Lk 2:34).

Through faith in Christ, many in and outside Israel will find redemption and new life in Him. But others, through their hard-heartedness and pride, opposed Him. As gentle and meek as Jesus is, because He is Truth Himself, there can never be neutrality or indecisiveness in our relationship with Him. "He that is not with Me, is against Me" (Mt 12:30).

The Church is a sign of contradiction against the world. The institution which Christ founded, the ark of salvation for all souls, like Himself, is a sign of contradiction to the wisdom of the world. It will meet the same rejection, the same opposition by the kingdom of the world. "If they persecuted Me, they will also persecute you" (Jn 15:20). It is enough to recall the great persecutions of the worldwide Church under the Roman Empire, Islam, Communism, and now, Western secularism, to see how much the Church has been hated for two thousand years.

Our life must be a contradiction against the world, and never a neutrality. The Christian vocation is to engage in the intense struggle between freedoms that are in mutual conflict. St. Augustine calls it a conflict of two loves: the love of God, to the point of disregarding self, or the love of self, to the point of disregarding God. "For we are to God the fragrance of Christ among those who are being saved and among those who are perishing. To the one we are the aroma of death leading to death, and to the other the aroma of life leading to life" (2 Co 2:15, 16).

PSALM 126 (127)

"If the Lord does not build the house, those who construct it labor in vain"

A certain woman passed away, leaving behind a young son and daughter. The husband was so attached to his wife that he used some magic and sorcery books to call up her spirit. One day, very strange noises came from their apartment. It sounded like dishes breaking and furniture crashing. This alarmed many of the tenants, not only from the same building, but even from neighboring buildings as well.

The man's two children were very frightened. He attempted on his own to dismiss the spirit several times, but it was all in vain. Nothing could be done and the condition of the apartment was a total disaster. All of the tenants as well as the neighbors in the whole area were frightened. Then, some people took the man to visit the monk, Fr. Mina the Solitary (St. Pope Kyrillos VI), who was living in Old Cairo.

The husband related his story to the monk, who then prayed over him for a long time. Fr. Mina then told him, "Don't ever do that again. Go home, and by the time you get there, everything will be over and done with."

Sure enough, before he got home, everything was calm, and the smell of incense was coming out of the apartment. All of the neighbors could smell it. From that moment on, all of their troubles were gone and the husband finally felt a sense of peace and consolation.

On Confession

Though we have received the grace of Baptism and Chrismation by which we have put on Christ and received the indwelling of the Holy Spirit, we remain free to cooperate or resist this grace. Knowing our feebleness, Christ has provided a remedy for the healing of sin and restoration in our life of grace. "Now all things are of God, who has reconciled us to Himself through Jesus Christ, and has given us the ministry of reconciliation" (2 Co 5:18).

It is true that God is not in need of our confession, for He knows the innermost part of our lives better than we do. Nonetheless, He established that the healing of our spiritual nature would depend on our accountability through confession. To Adam, after his disobedience, he asks, "Adam, where are you?...Did you eat of the tree?" And after Cain murdered his brother, Abel, "Cain, where is your brother Abel?"

This ministry of reconciliation, restoration, and healing is a gift to the Church. When Jesus healed the paralytic, He said, "But that you may know that the Son of Man has power on earth to forgive sins" (Mt 9:6). He uses the title "Son of Man," rather than "Son of God," to show that through His humanity, He gave humans power on earth, and this power is given to those who are called to the priesthood. "'As the Father has sent Me, I also send you.' And when He had said this, He breathed on them, and said to them, 'Receive the Holy Spirit. If you forgive the sins of any, they are forgiven them; if you retain the sins of any, they are retained.'" (Jn 20:21-23).

God has revealed the great power of the uttered word. That is why our healing from sin depends on not keeping it hidden which only further establishes us in our isolation. Through the encounter with divine mercy in the presence of the priest, we have the possibility of ending our isolation through the openness the Mystery (Sacrament) requires. The small shame we bear is of great consequence in uniting us to the shame of the Cross, which Christ bore and transformed by His Resurrection. When Christ stood before the Samaritan Woman, He said to her, "If you knew the gift of God, and who it is who says to you..." (Jn 4:10). Today, Christ, through His Church, is likewise asking us to recognize the gifts of His mercy, reconciliation, and healing through the Mystery of Confession.

PSALM 127 (128)

"Blessed are all who fear the Lord; who walk in His ways"

A certain young man used to visit Fr. Mina the Solitary (St. Pope Kyrillos VI) when he lived in the windmill near Old Cairo. In the summer of 1938, he went with another friend to visit Fr. Mina. While going up the mountain, they saw an old man with a walking stick who had a long beard and his hair was white like snow. The man asked them why they were going up the mountain as darkness was falling upon them. They told him that they were going to visit Fr. Mina in the windmill and he replied, "It is safe on the mountain. Have no fear and may the Lord be with you." He blessed them and left.

After only a few steps they looked behind them but there was no trace of the elder. They thought maybe he took a different route and was hidden behind the mountain tops. At the windmill, Fr. Mina welcomed them and then asked, "Did you see anybody on your way here?" Forgetting everything about the old man, they answered, "No." Fr. Mina asked again, "How come? Didn't you see an elder walking with a stick who asked you where you were going, and reassured you that it was safe on the mountain and then walked away?"

The two young men were surprised at his knowledge of all these details, and asked him who that person was. He asked them first if they knew who it was, and when they did not know the answer, he told them, "That was St. Paul the first Anchorite!"

On Progress in the Spiritual Life

Nothing seems more evident in the spiritual life than the obligation of seeking perfection. "Therefore you shall be perfect, just as your Father in heaven is perfect" (Mt 5:48). But not every good end begins with a good or pure intention. Sometimes hidden behind our desire to pursue perfection is a form of self-reliance. We want to become strong enough to establish some independence from God's mercy and grace. It is a refusal to accept poverty of spirit as the only acceptable means of spiritual growth, a lurking spiritual pride.

Our greatest safeguard is not our works but a pure desire born of love alone. The way of greater conversion and progress in love is to always recognize that we are in need of conversion. "Be converted to me with all your heart" (Joe 2:12). As one spiritual father reflected, every word and teaching of Christ is like a "Dart of Love" that pierces the heart toward greater conversion. Along the way, we must discern two traps that frustrate God's plan for our sanctity: despair and presumption.

Despair is the rejection of the truth that God desires and is willing to save us. The despairing soul believes salvation is impossible, thereby renouncing repentance and conversion. Despair is a form of self-love that refuses to acknowledge God as greater than our sin or weakness. It is unreservedly a sin against the goodness and mercy of God. St. John Climacus calls despair "spiritual suicide."

Presumption, on the other hand, is a false certitude of salvation that ignores the reverence due to God. Because it is not based on love, presumption uses the mercy of God as an excuse for sin and, therefore, lacks pain of heart over offenses against God. "How can you despise the riches of God's kindness and forbearance and patience? How can you fail to realize that His kindness is meant to lead you to repentance?" (Ro 2:4).

PSALM 128 (129)

"Never have my enemies prevailed against me"

A certain young man used to visit St. Mina's Church in Old Cairo from time to time to take the blessing of Fr. Mina the Solitary (St. Pope Kyrillos VI) before he was nominated as Patriarch. One night his visit extended past midnight and Fr. Mina suggested he stay the night since there was no transportation available. The young man apologized since he did not want to trouble or worry his family. However, the problem was that at this time there was a curfew imposed on the country so no one was allowed to walk in the streets.

After the young man insisted on leaving, Fr. Mina walked him outside and blessed him while saying, "Go. May St. Mina the Wonderworker be with you!"

Somehow, he walked from the Church to his house without incident. The amazing thing, however, was that he passed many soldiers along the way and they would salute him! At first he wondered why they would salute him, a civilian walking out in the streets after curfew. Then he realized they were saluting St. Mina who was accompanying him according to the words of Fr. Mina. Indeed St. Mina walked with him from the Church to his house in his military uniform as an officer.

On Discerning the Voice of the Holy Spirit

The spiritual life is a life led by the Holy Spirit. But how can we discern His voice among all the other competing voices around me and within me? Rare are the extraordinary manifestations of God's voice such as the conversion of St. Paul on the road to Damascus. Not only rare, but dangerous since we can become prey to the Devil who can masquerade as "an angel of light" (2 Co 11:14). The ordinary manner in the spiritual life is not through messages from heaven or visions, but rather through "an inner attraction" to that which the Holy Spirit is calling us to. Such attractions may at times be forceful, but more often they are quiet and discreet.

A first rule for discernment is whether the attraction is consistent with Holy Scriptures, the "mind" of Christ and the teachings of the Church. This, of course, requires us to be eager and diligent to merge our hearts with the heart of Christ and the Church, to align our spirit with the Spirit of Christ. Secondly, the Holy Spirit will not call us to respond to a demand that is excessive, either leading us toward pride or discouragement. Certainly, the grace of God elevates our human strength and makes us capable of heroic acts at times, but the usual means of inspiration are gradual and concrete, pointing to the moment by moment realities of our life. Third, God speaks through peace. This does not mean that He does not demand sacrifice, but that even great sacrifices with time and prayer are encompassed in a deep interior peace.

Finally, recourse to a spiritual director or confessor is an immense safeguard and source of grace, because we humble ourselves before another, thereby attracting God's grace, as well as turning to someone with spirit-filled experience and wisdom. Even in the case of St. Paul's extraordinary conversion, the Lord instructed him to go to a guide. "What shall I do, Lord?' And the Lord said to me, 'Arise and go into Damascus, and there you will be told all things which are appointed for you to do.'" (Ac 22:10).

The Twelfth Hour

PSALM 129 (130)

"Out of the depths I cry to You, O Lord; O Lord hear my voice"

The health of a certain man's son deteriorated terribly and he did not know what to do. He decided to visit St. Pope Kyrillos VI at the Patriarchate to ask for His Holiness' prayers and to have his son anointed with holy oil.

When he arrived, he was told that His Holiness was at the monastery for the next three weeks. The man was very upset. He stood in the church's courtyard and said, "I will ask God to heal my son." He went back to his house in Giza while praying, "You are the Healer of our souls and bodies." God heard his prayers and healed his son.

Two months later, the Saint was back from the monastery and the man went to take his blessings. When the Pope saw him, he said, "It is good, my son, that you asked God to heal your son. We too called upon God to answer your prayers. My thoughts were with you."

On Poverty of Spirit

"Blessed are the poor in spirit, for theirs is the kingdom of heaven" (Mt 5:3). This is the first of the beatitudes in the Sermon on the Mount. Many spiritual fathers consider it the source and door of all the other beatitudes, since it situates us in the most fundamental attitude that characterizes our filial relationship with God: childlike trust. On God's part, the poor, the weak, the miserable, and sinner, are the object of God's greater love. That is why the poor in spirit are "blessed." On man's part, poverty of spirit removes all our pretenses of our own strength and spiritual riches making us utterly dependent on God.

The word Jesus uses for "poor", *ptochos* in the original Greek, means someone who is completely destitute. Better translated as "beggar", it implies one who is completely dependent on someone else for support. The poor in spirit know that they are utterly destitute and helpless; only God's grace can clothe and sustain them. God is pleased with such a stance because it means He can give more generously when our hands are empty to receive Him. The poor in spirit are vulnerable, trusting, and devoid of all self-righteous pretentiousness; they surrender themselves totally to God.

Poverty of spirit secures and protects all of God's gifts under the mantle of humility. The poor in spirit cannot see or feel their virtue. They increase their repentance and tears because they are convinced by their own experience of poverty that they are the "chief sinner" (1 Ti 1:15). Their prayer is pure and pierces the heavens, like a starving beggar who by sheer necessity ardently begs for survival. Prayer becomes a conversation between two beggars. God begging for man to accept His gift of love, redemption, and salvation; and man whose cry surges from the depths of his distress.

PSALM 130 (131)

"O Lord, my heart is not proud nor are my eyes raised too high"

During the Vespers Raising of Incense service in Alexandria, while St. Pope Kyrillos VI began censing the church, a five-year-old boy began walking behind the Pope and kept stretching out his arms as if trying to catch a blessing. He was repeatedly rebuked by the people. However, he insisted on continuing to walk right behind the Pope, repeating the same gestures.

Even though the people continued to reprimand him, with great insistence he continued to walk directly behind the Saint. The Pope was immersed in prayer. When he came to notice how the people were severely admonishing the child behind him, he stated with tremendous kindness, "Leave him alone so that he might take a blessing."

At the end of the service they took the child aside in the presence of one of the priests, to speak with him and were surprised that the child said, "I was walking behind the angel who was walking behind Pope Kyrillos and I kept touching both of his beautiful wings." They glorified God who manifested how the heavens protected the Saint and how angels were his companions. The Saint knew what was happening but because of his humility said nothing about it.

On the Light of Christ

"I have come as a light into the world..." (Jn 12:46). The theme of light emerges dominantly in the teachings of Jesus. Without the light of the sun there would be no life. The association is clear; Jesus is the light of life and apart from Him we remain in darkness, which is eternal death. That is why He says that "he who does not believe is condemned already" (Jn 3:18). He is not making a moral judgement on His listeners that disbelief is just one among many sins. His statement is more poignant: to reject life is to embrace death.

Light has many properties and many effects. Light reveals and makes an object visible with clarity. Christ is the true Light in that He reveals both God and man. The Incarnation, Death, and Resurrection impart true knowledge about God, man, the world, and human destiny.

As God, Christ justifies God's love for man, and as Man, Christ justifies man's perfect obedience to God. The teachings and example of Christ's life are perfect illumination overcoming the darkness resulting from sin, death, and Satan.

Light exposes, much like a medical scan exposes a hidden cancer. His light exposes the hidden things of the heart, both good and evil. And just like a disease to be treated, it first has to be exposed for what it truly is, "for there is nothing covered that will not be revealed, and hidden that will not be known" (Mt 10:26). If the heart is not exposed and healed in this life, it will not escape its uncovering on the Day of Judgment. Light also warms. The light of Christ is pleasing, soothing, consoling, and inflames the human heart with divine love. "Did not our heart burn within us while He talked with us on the road?" (Lk 24:32). The warmth of Christ's light is perfect joy, peace, and satisfaction. Christ is also a guiding light for man in every detail of his earthly sojourn. "Your word is a lamp to my feet And a light to my path" (Ps 118:105). He is the Way (Jn 14:6).

PSALM 131 (132)

"Arise, O Lord, and go up to Your resting place"

Since Fr. Mina the Solitary (Pope Kyrillos VI) came to be the head of the Monastery of St. Samuel the Confessor for some time, a great love grew between him and Fr. Andrawis El-Samueli.

Fr. Andrawis said, "Pope Kyrillos VI stayed for some time with us in St. Samuel's Monastery during which period he was very pleasant and he loved me a great deal. He used to laugh with me and to take me with him to pray in the church. I used to call him "Our Master" (*Sayedna*), but he used to object by saying, "Why do you say, 'Our Master,' when you speak with me?" I would reply, "In the near future you will see that you will become [Our Master]. Pope Kyrillos left the monastery and I became very sad and wept at his departure. When he became the Patriarch, he visited St. Samuel's Monastery. When he saw me, he laughed and said, "Here, I have become 'Our Master' as you always called me and foretold in the past."

On Fr. Andrawis' first visit to St. Mina's Monastery while he was being medically treated in Alexandria, he went to the burial place of St. Pope Kyrillos VI. His face was radiating with joy while he was touching the marble of the grave. He kept kissing it many times, standing up to pray, and then repeating many times, "May his soul rest in peace." Afterwards he requested to sleep beside the grave of his beloved St. Pope Kyrillos, and so he was left alone for half an hour.

On the way back to Alexandria, Fr. Andrawis said to his disciple, "Father, I met with St. Pope Kyrillos in his shrine and talked with him." They were surprised and his disciple asked him what the Saint had told him. He replied, "While I was sleeping beside the burial place of Pope Kyrillos, he came to me and said, 'Have you come, my beloved?' I replied, 'If I am your beloved, ask Christ to call me to Him so that I may be comfortable beside you.' In his reply he said, 'It is not your turn, or time yet, Andrawis.' I then asked him to intercede and call me home to Paradise, but he firmly answered that I still had a long time to go."

One of the Alexandrian fathers who was in their company, stated, "Fr. Andrawis is going to live no less than five years as long as Pope Kyrillos made this comment to him." But Fr. Andrawis' physician did not take these words seriously as he knew how dire his medical condition was. In the end, what the Saint said was realized, and Fr. Andrawis lived for five more years.

On the Nature of Detachment

In the Ladder of Divine Ascent, St. John Climacus presents the spiritual life through the image of a ladder stretching from earth to heaven. Consisting of thirty rungs, the ladder he describes begins with the basic notion of conversion and commitment and then turns to the virtues and passions. He ends with the goal which is union with God. He places detachment on step two, a foundational point of conversion. Since detachment is a virtue, it is not inevitably related to a monastic vow. Detachment is not about physical poverty, it is a matter of the heart.

Detachment is not a scouring of creation, nor does it necessitate any dualism pitting the material against the spiritual, or the body against the soul. God created all things out of love and, therefore, all creation is inherently good. God is not in competition with His own creation. The problem of attachments is about misdirected priorities of love. "'Teacher, which is the great commandment in the law?' Jesus said to him, 'You shall love the Lord your God with all your heart, with all your soul, and with all your mind'" (Mt 22:36, 37).

When two people fall in love, naturally they become less interested or attracted to other people. Others are still good and beautiful, but now they are completely inferior to the love they have for each other. This was the experience of St. Paul: "More than that, I regard everything as loss because of the surpassing value of knowing Christ Jesus my Lord. For His sake I have suffered the loss of all things, and I regard them as rubbish, in order that I may gain Christ" (Php 3:8).

True asceticism begins in the heart and, only after, manifests itself outwardly through disciplines and mortifications. "We love Him because He first loved us" (1 Jn 4:19). This conflict begins in the heart if there is any tendency to seek satisfaction and fulfillment in substitutions: material things, earthly power, honors and titles, unhealthy relationships, and even certain spiritual experiences.

PSALM 132 (133)

"How wonderful and delightful it is for brothers to live together in unity"

A Roman Catholic priest from Shoubra had a heart attack and was admitted to the Italian Hospital. On the Nativity Feast in 1970, the doctors said his condition was critical and that he only had a few hours to live. According to Catholic tradition, in a situation like this the patient should receive last rites including Holy Communion.

Two acquaintances of the priest went together to visit him in the hospital and to check on his condition. One of them, upon seeing him, became distressed and kept weeping. The other friend suggested they go to St. Pope Kyrillos VI. They told the Pope about the priest's condition and added, "He is breathing his last and needs your blessing." The Pope asked them how old was the Father and was told he was about seventy-five years old. The Saint responded, "He is not old, he is still young." He then took a piece of hard candy, put it in his mouth and then took it out and said, "Take this, give it to him and let him suck on it and he will recover."

They rushed back to the hospital and although visitors were not allowed to see him, they managed to get the candy in the priest's mouth and he sucked on it.

How greatly the Lord was glorified! The priest recovered and gave thanks to God. He went to St. Pope Kyrillos VI, bowed before him in reverence and glorified the Lord.

On Detachment as Receptivity

Detachment is a liberation of the human heart in order to love God, others, and creation in the way intended from the beginning. The work of emptying is the path toward freeing the heart to love. It divests one of egoism in order to seek the good of the other. Our life seeks to glorify God and serve others out of love for Him. Detachment does not render us unresponsive to others. On the contrary, it allows us to be more attentive, more available, and more free to love them without any selfish motives or attachments.

Self-emptying makes possible the heart's capacity to become an inflow of God's life. He fills us to the extent we are empty. The Christian life is an imitation of Christ's own receptivity of the Father. "Then Jesus answered and said to them, 'Most assuredly, I say to you, the Son can do nothing of Himself, but what He sees the Father do; for whatever He does, the Son also does in like manner" (Jn 5:19). By doing the Father's will, Jesus gives us a demonstration of perfect human freedom. He is free to do the Father's will because He does not have an opposing will. When we cling to our attachments by our own will, we impede God's will for us which is always the best and most perfect thing for us at any moment.

The Church affords us the opportunity to practice detachment through the discipline of fasting. True detachment means we begin to let go of our preferences or, at least, we are not crippled by our preferences. Through fasting we learn to live on a deeper level than that of preferences. Inordinate possessions and preferences will always mean greater anxiety. "Again, the kingdom of heaven is like a merchant seeking beautiful pearls, who, when he had found one pearl of great price, went and sold all that he had and bought it" (Mt 13:45, 46).

PSALM 133 (134)

"Lift up your hands toward the sanctuary and bless the Lord"

While a certain woman was in the kitchen preparing breakfast for her children, a pot containing boiling oil spilled on her arm. In severe pain, she started screaming. Her arm instantly turned red and she was unable to move it. She tried several ointments but the inflammation started spreading to her chest.

She went to a physician who told her it was necessary to remove an abscess in her armpit. She was upset because she did not know who would take care of her children while she had the operation. She heard that St. Pope Kyrillos VI was visiting a nearby Church and decided to go and ask for his prayers.

Her arm was so swollen that she had to put it into a sling. Even though she was in severe pain, she was forced to carry her toddler. When they arrived at the church, a big crowd surrounded His Holiness. She did not approach him, afraid somebody would bump into her arm, and so she was unable to meet him.

However, as they began to walk home, they saw Pope Kyrillos' car stop a few steps away from them. His face was lit up with grace. They quickly approached the car and she asked the Saint to pray for her. He looked at her and placed the Cross on her arm saying, "May the Lord bless you, my daughter, and heal you." They only walked a few meters when fluid gushed onto her clothes from under her arm. She was able to move her arm freely and her arm was back to its normal color and size!

Later she went to see the surgeon who was going to perform the operation. When he saw her arm, he was greatly astonished and said, "This is definitely a miracle. All things are possible with the Lord!"

On Contemplation in the World

The word "contemplation" means the act of looking upon or gazing attentively. It is a way of "seeing". In the spiritual life, it encompasses a silent and loving way of seeing God in the world. By virtue of our baptism, all Christians are called to live as contemplatives, meaning to recognize God's presence and love in everything around us. In contemplative prayer, the focus might be more inwardly-directed - a silent and loving conversation with the Lord in our hearts - but a contemplative perspective extends to the outside world as well. "For with You is the fountain of life; in Your light we see light" (Ps 35:9).

The more the soul lives in contemplation, the more it will love God and be inspired to greater generosity toward the world and one's neighbor. The Mother of God is the model of a contemplative soul that reaches the highest degree of care for the world. She desires and intercedes to direct all of humanity to her Son and eternal life. By consenting to become His mother, she accepted to become a mother to all the redeemed. This calling to embrace the world in one's heart and affections, to pray and work for the salvation of others, is the fruit of a truly contemplative life.

A deep eucharistic life is always contemplative as we perceive the outpouring of God's love hidden in the bread and wine. Likewise, when Jesus said, "The poor you will always have with you" (Mk 14:7), it was not a matter of the impossibility of eradicating the problem of poverty, but rather that we would always find Him in what Mother Theresa of Calcutta called "the distressing disguise of the poor". A contemplative soul is one that seeks and finds God's presence hidden behind the guise of the world and in other people. His presence is always a gift of His love.

PSALM 136 (137)

"If I forget you, O Jerusalem, may my right hand fail me"

A certain couple was married in February 1959 and the wife became pregnant soon after. Their relatives convinced them to have an abortion since they were still young and not ready for the responsibility. Because they were far from God, they were easily convinced of the idea and the wife had the abortion.

Later, they longed to have a child but could not. Even after seeing many doctors, there was no change. In 1962, a friend advised them to go see St. Pope Kyrillos VI.

They went to see the Pope and knelt down before him, telling him their story. He said, "Don't you know that what you did is a great sin? It is murder, how could you do that? May the Lord forgive you but you have to repent. You have to offer a truthful penitence to God and fast for three days." They then asked him to pray for them the Absolution. He did, blessed them, and said, "You will have children soon."

Nine months after seeing the Saint, the wife gave birth to twins.

On God's Justice

The theme of God's justice makes up a big part of the Old Testament. God's justice manifests an attentiveness to human need. God is a defender of "the widow, the orphan, the traveler, and the stranger..." (*Divine Liturgy of St. Basil*) "He administers justice for the fatherless and the widow, and loves the stranger, giving him food and clothing" (Dt 10:18). Fundamental to God's nature is His defense of the defenseless. Because injustices were rampant among His people, God rejected their worship and chastised them:

> 'Yes, they surpass the deeds of the wicked; they do not plead the cause, the cause of the fatherless; yet they prosper, and the right of the needy they do not defend. Shall I not punish them for these things?' says the Lord. 'Shall I not avenge Myself on such a nation as this?' (Je 5:28, 29).

But where do we lay the blame? Where is the line of demarcation between the just and unjust? As Isaiah declared, "We have all become like one who is unclean, And all our righteousnesses are like filthy rags"

(Is 64:6) None are pure and without blame for contributing to the injustices in the world. We are all victims and victimizers. Only God Who took flesh without sin, can offer an answer, a solution to injustice: "The destruction decreed shall overflow with righteousness" (Is 10:22). The sacrifice of Christ declares that there is no human solution, nothing from within the sphere of human influence that can solve the problem.

The Cross is the meeting of destruction and righteousness: destruction because Christ took upon Himself all the injustices of the world, and righteousness because there is a new creation. He suffered the condemnation of a criminal on behalf of all humanity, and He is raised to proclaim the justice of God. The justice of God, in Christ, was not the punishment of humanity, but a new creation and a new existence in Christ. "Therefore, if anyone is in Christ, he is a new creation; old things have passed away; behold, all things have become new" (2 Co 5:17).

PSALM 137 (138)

"The day in which I call upon You, hear me speedily and look upon my soul with power"

A certain young man was going into the army and was so scared that he suffered a mental breakdown. He tried seeing many psychiatrists to no avail, so they decided to have the army doctor check him out so they could clear him from the service due to his condition. On the way to Cairo where he would see the army doctor, the young man repeatedly tried to jump out the window. Unfortunately, once there, the doctor said they were only seeing people from another province.

The first week of October 1970, his relative took him to visit St. Pope Kyrillos VI and take his blessing. When their turn in line was coming up, the Saint called the relative by name and told him to come forward. They approached and the young man immediately knelt down on his knees and the Saint blessed him.

The Saint then told him, "Get up, you are now awake; go back to work and don't be afraid." And exactly as the Saint declared, he got up looking like a different person, like he was before his breakdown. Since then, he did very well working in the army.

On Meditating on God's Love

The modern Greek Elder Porphyrios of Kafsokalivia summarized the spiritual struggle as taking one of two directions. The first, he said, was to focus on fighting against sin and the passions. The second, by loving Christ and His will. He concluded by saying that the former achieves little because it becomes a cold and hard struggle, while the latter achieves more because by loving Christ, sin loses its appeal and influence. To dispel the darkness it is better to simply let the light in.

St. John the Apostle states, "We love Him because He first loved us" (1 Jn 4:19). Perfection consists in loving God. This is why St. Augustine said, "Love God, and do what you will." Those who love God will not do anything that displeases love. Therefore, it is profitable for us to routinely meditate on God's love for us, so that His love can inflame our own love for Him and others. "Yes, I have loved you with an everlasting love; therefore with lovingkindness I have drawn you" (Je 31:3). God's love is conveyed in His creating us, redeeming us, and saving us.

Reflect on the creation of which you are the pinnacle of His handiwork. You bear His image and likeness, which the sun, the moon, the stars, the oceans, and the mountains, in all their glory do not. Everything was created for your enjoyment and pleasure. Though sin and death despoiled God's original design, remember always the Passion of Christ and the cost of your redemption. How powerful are the Holy Week services of our church in arousing in us a sense of loving contrition for our sins that put Him on the Cross. "Having loved His own who were in the world, He loved them to the end" (Jn 13:1). Having forgiven us and redeemed through love, trampling over sin, death, and Satan, He calls us to the heights of glory and sanctity. To sanctify us, He established for us the Church and the Sacrament of His love, the Eucharist. Along with all the other sacraments, this one is especially stamped with intimacy, friendship, companionship, and humble condescension. Recall every day the manner of your creation, redemption, and sanctification and it will always steer you to the love of God.

PSALM 140 (141)

"Let my prayer be set forth before You as incense, and the lifting up of my hands like the evening sacrifice"

In 1963, a certain woman's son was born, bringing great joy to the family. Unfortunately, for some reason he refused to eat and his health deteriorated rapidly. Several professors from the Faculty of Medicine at the University of Alexandria examined him, but were unable to diagnose the underlying cause. They decided to have a team of specialists examine him, with the hopes that they could reach a diagnosis.

While the mother was waiting in the hospital for the consultation, she heard that St. Pope Kyrillos VI was at St. Mark's Cathedral in Alexandria. Without thinking twice, she took her son and headed to the Cathedral. The mother was in despair when she saw such a large crowd around the Pope. However, to her surprise, she saw the Saint gesturing for her to come close. "You, little boy with the hat, come here." He then asked the crowd to make room for the mother and before she could say a word, he comforted her, "Don't cry. The boy is just fine!"

He then blew into the boy's face and blessed him while placing the Cross on his head. Turning to the mother, he said, "You don't have to go back to the hospital, just go home. The boy is fine." The mother was amazed that the Saint knew everything without her telling him anything.

As soon as the mother arrived home, she started feeding the boy who eagerly drank all the milk she gave him. Later that day, the mother's brother (who is a physician) visited them and reprimanded her for leaving the hospital and missing the consultation. He then insisted on taking the boy to a friend of his who was one of the professors who previously examined him. After he completed the checkup, the professor's only comment was, "I know for a fact that you folks [i.e., Christians] have miracles that are beyond understanding."

On Inner Peace

Tranquility, harmony, order, and serenity are all characteristics of peace. Peace is the legacy of the Savior and our inheritance. One of the first proclamations ushering in the Good News of the Gospel was that of God's peace. "And suddenly there was with the angel a multitude of the heavenly host praising God and saying: 'Glory to God in the highest, and on earth peace, goodwill toward men!'" (Lk 2:13, 14). It is the peace of reconciliation with God and the gift of Jesus to the world. "For He Himself is our peace" (Eph 2:14).

The peace Christ offers the believer is something utterly capable of withstanding all external disturbances. We cannot change the world or people around us as a precondition for peace. The original state of man was one of inner peace and harmony. Thus, inner peace is directly related to communion with God. It is an altogether different kind of peace than the peace the world can offer. Christ's peace is a divine gift: "...a peace the world cannot give, this is My gift to you" (Jn 14:27). Likewise, as we pray in the Divine Liturgy, "You have filled the earth with the heavenly peace..."

From a divine standpoint, then, peace is fundamentally related to sin and the disordered passions. Since self-love is the source of the passions, it also follows that peace is the fruit of Christ-like humility, as Jesus said, "Take My yoke upon you and learn from Me, for I am gentle and lowly in heart, and you will find rest for your souls" (Mt 11:29).

The door to the passions are the bodily senses; they are gateways to the soul. Though sin ordinarily seeks entrance through the fives senses (sight, hearing, taste, smell, and touch), it can also come through demonic suggestion, our own imaginations, and memory (the remembrance of evil). The loss of our inner peace leads to fear, sadness, worry, anger, frustration, loss of hope, and depression. Inversely, without peace, it is impossible to acquire other virtues. Among the virtues that most perfectly gives birth to peace is that of trust in God. When we align our will with God's will and entrust our future to Him, peace will reign in our hearts. "Be anxious for nothing, but in everything by prayer and supplication, with thanksgiving, let your requests be made known to God; and the peace of God, which surpasses all understanding, will guard your hearts and minds through Christ Jesus" (Php 4:6, 7).

PSALM 141 (142)

"Rescue me from those who seek to persecute me, for they are too strong for me"

St. Pope Kyrillos VI was visiting the city of Beheira. Because of the Saint's reputation for sanctity, large crowds of both Christians and Muslims participated in a glorious reception, and many reported that they saw a halo of light surrounding the Pope's head.

The city's assistant district attorney said that his brother-in-law, a non-Christian, disliked the magnificent reception the Pope received and criticized the excessive welcoming of this Christian leader. The assistant district attorney said, "I assured him that the people's response was spontaneous and no previous arrangements were made." Early the next morning, the man was awakened by his brother-in-law who looked terrified. He told him that the Pope reproached him in a dream saying, "Are you upset because they cheered a little for the Christian leader? Don't be upset!"

The brother-in-law asked him to accompany him to the Saint to ask for his forgiveness. They were very surprised that the Pope, although he didn't know them, said, "Are you upset because they cheered a little for the Christian leader? Don't be upset!" Astonished, they asked for his forgiveness. He then prayed for them and blessed them.

On Prudence

Aristotle defined "virtue" as "that which makes both a person and what he does good." Virtue can exist at a natural level whereby one makes an effort and perseveres in choosing to do good. But there also exists a supernatural level of virtue in which divine grace comes to man's aid in overcoming his sinful nature and raising him to Christ-like stature.

The virtue of prudence is doing the right thing, at the right time, in the right measure. St. Augustine said of it, "Prudence is the knowledge of what to seek and what to avoid." It is the right way to arrive at a good end. At the natural level, prudence is good common sense and solid judgment. At the supernatural level, it is directly related to doing God's will, which results in the best temporal and eternal consequences. With the aid of divine grace, prudence enables us to act in accordance with the Gospel. "But the natural man does not receive the things of the Spirit of God... But we have the mind of Christ" (1 Co 2:14, 16).

From an earthly perspective, living according to the Gospel will often seem imprudent. We can take the example of the martyrs who laid down their temporal lives in exchange for the glory of eternal life. The reverse is likewise true. Many of the choices we make, which the world praises and embraces, are imprudent in terms of their consequences on our eternal life. We can easily think of the many passions of the flesh. "Those who live according to the flesh fix their attention on the things of the flesh, while those who live according to the Spirit set their thoughts on spiritual things" (Ro 8:5).

To practice godly prudence we need to first be formed in the Truth. It is not enough to have a "good" conscience, we must have an "informed" conscience by the Holy Spirit. "We have not received the spirit of the world but the Spirit who is from God, so that we may understand the gifts bestowed upon us by God" (1 Co 2:12). In addition to possessing the truth, we need patience and endurance to overcome all the obstacles Satan and the world will set before us, remembering that the final good we seek is union with God.

PSALM 145 (146)

"The Lord gives wisdom to the blind; the Lord loves the righteous"

A certain young man first met St. Pope Kyrillos VI in 1969. At that time he was in the second year of secondary school. He was raised in a Protestant family which did not believe in the intercession of saints. He had epilepsy and dozens of physicians could not help him. He was prescribed medication and electroconvulsive therapy, all to no avail.

In a very short time, he had accumulated at least fifty prescriptions and electroencephalograms and doctors were puzzled by his condition for about two years. In the winter of 1969, they were in Cairo for treatment. His uncle and his sister suggested that they go see St. Pope Kyrillos VI, but his parents refused this idea, and it was only after much insistence that his parents accepted, against their will, to go with them.

The Pope had a very beautiful and unforgettable smile on his face, and without knowing them before, he addressed the father saying, "Kiss the Cross, you Protestant, and don't kiss my hand." He told them that they came from Upper Egypt and looked at the mother saying, "Where are Dr. (the brother's name) and Eng. (the other brother's name)?" The two brothers were not with them during the visit. One was eight years old at that time and the other fourteen years old (this was a prophecy by the Saint).

Then His Holiness looked at the young man smiling, and pointing at him with his Cross, said, "Come," and he put the Cross on his forehead and said, "You are not sick, it's over, you are OK." This happened without anyone telling him that he was sick! They left astonished by the deep spirituality of the Saint and stopped all of the treatment when they returned to Assiut. From that day on he did not suffer any epileptic fits, and the prophecy concerning the two brothers was fulfilled; one of them became a surgeon and the other a civil engineer!

On Meekness

"Go! I am sending you out like lambs among wolves" (Lk 10:3). These words of Jesus characterize what a disciple's heart must be like, in order to mirror the Lord's own heart. The disciple must proclaim the Gospel not by imposition or force, but meekly through goodness and humility, honoring the freedom of the other. Meekness and humility (Mt 11:28) most consummately depict the heart of Jesus. "Now I, Paul, myself am pleading with you by the meekness and gentleness of Christ—who in presence am lowly among you..." (2 Co 10:1). Meekness is a quality that incorporates gentleness, restraint, goodness, patience, humility, self-possession and non-violence.

Meekness is not weakness or cowardice. It is not a passive attribute to be meek, but one actively born out of strength and self-mastery. "Remember, O Lord, David and his meekness" (Ps 131:1). King David is praised for his meekness because in his strength, he practiced humble restraint (1 Sa 24) against Saul for the sake of goodness and love of God. The meek always work toward the aim of building up and not destroying. Jesus' meekness is manifest in His masterful dealings with those on the brink. "A bruised reed he will not break, and a dimly burning wick he will not quench" (Is 42:3; Mt 12:20). His meeting with the Samaritan Woman (Jn 4) and the manner in which He extricated the woman caught in adultery (Jn 8) communicated the honor He conferred on every human soul.

There are people who appear to have a naturally meek disposition to their personalities. Typically, this is as long as everything goes well with them. But when serious adversity or opposition touches them they may become like burning coals hidden under ashes. The meekness of the saints is a supernatural virtue because it is elevated by divine grace and tied inseparably to the virtue of faith. A desert elder noticed that someone in the night was stealing from him his handiwork. Staying awake and hiding one night to see who it was, he was surprised to discover it was his young disciple. He did nothing, and years later, when the elder was dying, he asked that his disciple be brought to him. The elder grabbed hold of the young monk's hand and began kissing it. When they inquired why he was doing this, he replied that he was kissing the hand that opened for him the door to Paradise.

PSALM 146 (147)

"He heals the brokenhearted and bandages their wounds"

A certain woman's parents had been separated since she was a child. She used to live with her mother and never knew her father because she never saw him during her childhood. In 1964, she reached the legal age that permitted her father to force her under his custody, which he did with the help of the police authorities.

After moving to her father's house to live with his non-Christian wife, he forbade her to visit her mother or even call her on the phone. This was a very painful situation which made her always sad. She once asked her father permission to visit her mother with tears and, only after some relatives intervened, did he allow her to, with the condition that she would not ask again.

During the visit to her mother, they went to see St. Pope Kyrillos VI who was at the Cathedral of St. Mark in Alexandria at that time. As usual, there was a large number of visitors asking for the Saint's blessing. When it was their turn, the mother explained her case to the Saint and asked for his prayers for her daughter. The Saint put his hand over her head and prayed a long prayer. He then said to the mother, "Don't worry, your daughter will return to you."

On the same day, immediately upon her return to her father's house, the father asked her, "Do you want to go to your mother?" She replied, "Yes", so he said, "Go to her and remain there." Since that time she has lived with her mother.

On Compassion for Others

"When the Lord saw her, He had compassion on her" (Lk 7:13). The word "compassion" means "to suffer with". Christian compassion is co-suffering with another. "Rejoice with those who rejoice, and weep with those who weep" (Ro 12:15).

Elder Paisios of Mount Athos described the Christian as a "mass of pain". We cannot love, pray or serve unless our hearts are filled with compassion for others. That means that we are called to carry with us the pain that exists in the world and in the hearts of others. A young lady who was once physically beaten by her older brother, ran out of her house and went straight to the Patriarchate to see St. Pope Kyrillos VI. As soon as the Saint saw her, he said, "I was there with you and I received every blow with you!"

Suffering with others for the sake of Christ is not a depressive state. Since it is born out of divine love, God consoles the soul and gives it joy. Christ and the saints truly feel the pain of the world but they remain full of tranquility and joy. If being compassionate causes us to remain in prolonged sadness or anxiety, it means our compassion is purely human and has not been united to faith and hope.

Our own suffering fashions us to be more sensitive, expanding our heart, to feel the pain of others and console them. "He consoles us in our affliction and thereby enables us to console others in their tribulations, offering them the consolation with which we ourselves are consoled by God" (2 Co 1:4).

And likewise, through love for the person, we forget our own sufferings when we feel the pain of others. Compassion enables us to see past the external faults of others, even the ones that directly hurt us, because we feel their underlying pain which is the source of their actions. This is how God deals with the soul. That is why judgment is so despised by God, because only He knows the situation, environment, and strength of each person. "Rather, be kind to one another and compassionate, and forgive one another as God has forgiven you in Christ" (Eph 4:32).

PSALM 147 (147)

"He sends His word to the earth: His word runs swiftly"

In 1969, a certain priest from Fayoum experienced a paralysis of his tongue for more than six months. Many doctors treated him but the Lord did not grant him healing.

At that time, his son, who was also later ordained a priest, was a lecturer of medicine at the university. He frequently visited St. Pope Kyrillos VI, and in one of those visits he said to the Saint, "Your Holiness, I'm sad for my father, he is sick. Please utter a word of prayer from your pure mouth so that God may grant him healing."

The Saint prayed for the priest and gave him a piece of cotton anointed with holy oil and a piece of holy bread and said, "Rest assured, your father will be healed by the blessings of the Lord and the prayers of His saints."

His son brought the cotton with oil and the priest motioned for him to anoint his tongue. After he did, he took a nap, and when he woke up he felt a great change. He was healed and could speak again.

On the Sanctification of Time

"Make the most of the present time, for this is a wicked age" (Eph 5:16), St. Paul wrote to the Ephesians. Time is a gift from God given to us to mature into "the measure of the stature of the fullness of Christ" (Eph 4:13). The Lord Jesus Christ Himself as Man "increased in wisdom and in stature" (Lk 2:52), exhibiting God's will for man's use of time. Further, the thirty years of Jesus' obscurity in Nazareth is a display of a wise application of time.

The Church has always understood that it exists in time, between the "fullness of time" (Ga 4:4) of Christ's first coming and the "end of the age" (Mt 28:20) when Christ will come in His glory to judge the living and the dead. The Church now lives in the power of the Holy Spirit to proclaim the Good News, to sanctify souls and to prepare the world for Christ's return. Sanctification is the work appropriated to the Holy Spirit. To sanctify is to "set apart" and "make holy". Like all gifts from God, time must be set apart for God and consecrated to Him.

Our experience of time is both cyclical and linear. Cyclical time is what we see on our calendars, a repetition of hours, days, weeks, months, and years. Linear time can be characterized by our birth, growth, aging, and death. It is the latter that perhaps gives us the greatest sense of the precious nature of time. The sanctification of time, then, is the association of both cyclical and linear time with the mystery of Christ—His life, death, and resurrection. The Church affords us the possibility of sanctifying cyclical time through the annual cycle of feasts and fasts. The week is sanctified by the Lord's Day on Sunday. The day is sanctified by the Prayers of the Hours (*Agpeya*), daily commemorations and liturgies. Every second can be sanctified by prayer: "Lord Jesus have mercy on me!"

Linear time is also sanctified. It is sanctified in birth through the Mysteries of Holy Baptism and Chrismation, in growth and aging through the Mysteries of the Eucharist and Confession, and in other Mysteries that aid us in fulfilling God's will, such as Marriage and Ordination. Linear time is finally sanctified as we approach the deterioration of the body and death in the spiritual healing found in the Mystery of Holy Unction. "Teach us to comprehend how few our days are so that our hearts may be filled with wisdom" (Ps 89:12).

THE MIDNIGHT HOUR

PSALM 118-1 (119)

"O that my ways were directed to keep Your ordinances"

A certain man's friend did not believe in miracles nor in the sanctity of St. Pope Kyrillos VI. One day, the man told his friend to join him in going to see the Pope and he reluctantly agreed after much nagging.

The Saint blessed the unbelieving man and struck him on his back with the Cross. The doubtful man was not happy about this and questioned why the Saint did this. His friend did not know, but felt there must be some reason behind the Saint's actions.

When the unbelieving man returned home, he was surprised that he was able to take his jacket off easily, since, prior to that, he was suffering from severe rheumatism in his back and always had difficulty removing his jacket.

The Saint knew this man's suffering and prayed for his cure, even though he was skeptical and did not want to see him.

On Obedience

Obedience is the surrender of our will to God's will, as revealed by the commandments in the Word of God, the Church's precepts, and through all godly obligations associated with our state in life. As we progress further in adhering to the will of God, the Holy Spirit will inspire us to make additional acts of obedience in order to achieve our perfect union with God.

In the miracle of the great catch of fish (Lk 5:1-11), we discover a progression of obedience leading to greater faith and adherence to Christ in the life of St. Peter. First, Peter heard the word of God being taught (Lk 5:3). Secondly, he obeyed the command of the Lord to launch into the deep (Lk 5:5). And last, he left all and surrendered his whole life to Christ (Lk 5:11). Jesus enters Peter's life gradually, asking of him a greater commitment each time. The Lord does the same with each of us throughout the course of our lives. Even if we miss His visitations in the hidden circumstances of daily life, we meet Him weekly in the Eucharist. We should ask ourselves at every Holy Communion what sacrifice and obedience Christ is seeking from us.

Similar to the beatitudes in the Sermon on the Mount, Jesus ascribes "blessedness" to obedience. "...blessed are those who hear the word of God and keep it!" (Lk 11:28). This "blessedness" is an identification of intimacy with Jesus. "Who is My mother, or My brothers? For whoever does the will of God is My brother and My sister and mother" (Mk 3:33, 35).

Man's greatest gifts are his free will and reason. Through obedience, we offer both to God as a pleasing sacrifice. It is allowing our life to be ruled by another, and, in the case of obedience to God, that means He will govern our life toward perfect joy and satisfaction. Obedience is the quickest way to perfection and union with God, since it secures us firmly in the Divine Will. For "whoever does the will of God abides forever" (1 Jn 2:17).

PSALM 118-2 (119)

"I have hidden Your words in my heart, that I might not sin against You"

A certain woman knew Fr. Mina the Solitary (St. Pope Kyrillos VI) since he was in the Windmill and attended many services with him receiving his blessings.

In 1956, she was a senior in the American University studying physiology and sociology while working as an art teacher. One day she decided to paint a picture of St. Mina the Wonderworker and wanted to discuss the project with Fr. Mina at his church in Old Cairo. She had some lectures at the university first and was carrying many heavy books with her. When she was crossing the railroad tracks close to one of the stations, she looked both ways to be sure no train was coming. Seeing nothing, she advanced slowly because there was a lot of gravel between the rails. Suddenly she felt a strong push forcing her to fall to the ground. Within a second, a train passed less than one foot away from her. It seemed that the station building obstructed her view.

She was very frightened and upset at the realization that she was so close to death and thought to herself, "What kind of reward is that for someone who wanted to do something good?!" She reached the church limping due to the fall.

Fr. Mina came walking toward her, holding water in one hand and a bottle of oil in the other. He was smiling and then said, "Is this the reward for someone who wants to do something good?!" as if he was playing back a tape recorder. She was puzzled by what she was hearing and seeing. Then he said, "Come, blessed one. What did St. Mina do to you? Did he push you to the ground? He reached you before the train was going to hit you. He saved you because he wants you to paint the picture for us. He will also heal your leg so that there will be no scars."

He prayed over the water and blessed it three times before sprinkling it on her face three times. He also poured the oil he had on her head until it ran down her face and neck. She had forgotten the tape measure that she needed back in her desk and Fr. Mina even knew about this. He told her, "'You forgot the tape measure and only brought your books, but I have the measurement you need." He gave her a string with two knots which corresponded exactly to the correct dimensions for the painting.

On Envy

Whereas jealousy is the desire to possess that which another has, envy is the sadness or anger felt along with the wish that the other be deprived of it. Envy rejoices at another's loss. It begins with jealousy as a weakness, and ends with envy as deep sadness and malice. The envious person, St. Basil the Great says, sees the good fortune of his neighbor as his own affliction. Other passions have some pleasure associated with them, but envy is called by the saints the most joyless of sins, and the sin without limits.

Envy is born of pride. Our pride whispers to us that we should be the sole bearers of all the gifts, talents, and possessions of others. It is not limited to material things and earthly honors, for envy can be at its worst when we despise others for their spiritual experiences and gifts. "Prove by your good life that your works are done with the humility that comes from wisdom...But if your hearts are filled with bitter envy and selfish ambition...Such wisdom does not come down from above, but is earthly, unspiritual and demonic...there will be disharmony and every type of wickedness" (Jas 3:13-15).

Humility will lead us to accept that God has given us precisely what we need for our salvation, and that possessing someone else's gifts would be our demise. It is not through great works or talents that the saints reached the height of sanctity, but in a life of surrender and acceptance of God's will in everything. The saints also rejoiced in the gifts and talents of others for they were only concerned about the glory of God. They comprehend the mystery of the Church as Head with a Body, and that every talent and grace given to one is the possession, and for the benefit, of all. No sin more closely makes us resemble Satan than envy. For it was "the envy of the Devil" (Wis 2:24) that brought about his own fall and the fall of the first man.

PSALM 118-3 (119)

"Unveil my eyes that I may clearly see the wonders to be found in Your law"

A certain man was born in 1956, the youngest and only son, with three sisters. When he was three years old, his parents noticed that he was unable to get out of bed and was also unable to move his left foot. He was seen by several doctors and was diagnosed with polio. The news was devastating for the family.

He was taken to a specialist in Cairo who confirmed the diagnosis of polio and told the parents that there was no cure for this disease. All that could be done was physical therapy as well as putting his leg between bags of sand to avoid curvature of the bone. This was done to prepare for the mounting of a metal device for the left foot.

After his ordination in 1959, St. Pope Kyrillos VI came to Tanta for a pastoral visit. He visited almost all the churches of the diocese. Because the Pope had a reputation of being a saintly person with the gift of performing miracles, the crowds around him were intense. His mother was carrying him in her arms and tried following the Saint everywhere he went trying to meet him but she could not. At the end of his tour of the diocese, he visited the Cathedral of St. George, but again, the crowd was so intense that the mother lost all hope of meeting the Saint. She headed toward one of the side altars in order to exit the church from the door where the baptistry room was. As soon as she walked into that area, she was surprised to see His Holiness right in front of her! He, too, was about to exit the church from that same side door in order to avoid the heavy crowd. She immediately asked him to pray for her son who was suffering from polio. He laid his hand over his head and prayed, and then said, "Do not be afraid. He will recover and he will be just fine."

A few days later, the boy woke up in the morning able to move his left foot. He was able to get out of bed all by himself and move around normally. The parents took him to the same specialist in Cairo who was quite astonished. He said, "This is the first time I have seen anyone recover from polio. All I was going to do was prepare him for the brace. There is no treatment of any kind for this disease!"

On the Difficulties of Faith

"And without faith it is impossible to please God, because anyone who comes to Him must believe that He exists and that He rewards those who earnestly seek Him" (Heb 11:6). Believing that God exists, along with the truths of the faith as recited in the Christian Creed, is foundational to a life of faith. But mature faith penetrates every aspect of one's life. Faith can never be a mere intellectual assent of the mind. It must continually undergo a martyrdom of the mind and a heart growing in the trust and confidence of a child's heart. Along this journey there will be many difficulties, purifications, and questions that will challenge our confidence in God and tempt us to abandon the progress of faith. St. Peter wrote that genuine faith will be "tested by fire" (1 Pe 1:7).

As one spiritual father noted, faith does not remove darkness–it requires it. To grow in faith is to accept mystery and insecurity, and, yet, to go on trusting and loving God. The mystery of God will constantly challenge what we thought we knew about God, what ideas we formed about Him, and what we expected from Him. At times, our lives will be turned upside down with nothing to support us but our decision to keep in the goodness and faithfulness of God. Even many of the great saints were left without answers to their cries. St. Antony the Great questioned God about all the injustices of the world and God's reply to him was, "Antony, keep your attention on yourself; these things are according to the judgment of God, and it is not to your advantage to know anything about them."

A priest went to India to seek the advice of Mother Teresa of Calcutta on a significant matter of discernment in his ministry. When she asked him what he wanted her to pray for, he replied, "Clarity." She responded firmly by telling him that she would not pray for him to have greater clarity, but rather greater trust. She wanted to say that clarity is often a cloak for fear of trusting. Faith requires that we let go of the craving for security.

PSALM 118-4 (119)

"I ran in the way of Your commandments, when You enlarged my heart"

A close friend of St. Pope KyrillosVI, a deacon, once served the Vespers Raising of Incense service with the Saint along with another monk, who was reciting the congregational responses with the congregation. During the Doxologies, the Pope stood quietly in the Sanctuary, but suddenly a wide smile appeared on his face and he laughed. It was a sight that shocked the deacon, since knowing the Saint for so many years, he knew how strict the Pope was with himself and others while inside the Sanctuary.

He asked him after the service the reason for his laughter inside the Sanctuary but the Saint attempted to avoid his question. Upon the deacon's persistence, the Saint promised to tell him with the condition of not mentioning anything about the incident until his passing. He said, "When I entered the Sanctuary, I was deeply troubled by an issue related to the Copts. Suddenly, St. Mina appeared to me and asked why I was distressed. When I explained the reason, he responded, 'Do you think you are alone? We are all here supporting you.' Then, he (St. Mina) lightly pushed me and so I laughed.'"

On Spiritual Reading

Spiritual reading immerses our mind and heart in the knowledge of God, giving us a foundation for prayer and loving God. Our readings should consist primarily of the Holy Scriptures, the lives of the saints, spirituality, dogma, and life within the church. Spiritual reading has led many to conversion of life, and for others it is daily nourishment on divine truth leading to greater faith, hope and love.

Love proceeds from knowledge; we love someone when we get to know them, and in loving them we want to know more about them. "And this is eternal life, that they may know You, the only true God, and Jesus Christ whom You have sent" (Jn 17:3). When the heart is inflamed by love, it longs and yearns through greater inquiry toward its object. Faith is sustained by truth, both dogmatic truths and the experiential, or practical, truths of the saints. "How then shall they call on Him in whom they have not believed? And how shall they believe in Him of whom they have not heard? And how shall they hear without a preacher?" (Ro 10:14).

With the regular practice of spiritual reading, the soul becomes consistently occupied with God, leading it into greater depths of prayer in an atmosphere of silence and solitude. St. Isaac the Syrian says that through spiritual reading the soul is enlightened in prayer. And Elder Paisios of Mount Athos calls spiritual reading the fortifying vitamins of the soul. Without good spiritual reading, we risk a spirituality of excessive sentimentality or a secularization of Christian life which ultimately leaves the soul unaffected. "The good man brings good things out of the good stored up in his heart, and the evil man brings evil things out of the evil stored up in his heart. For out of the overflow of his heart, his mouth speaks" (Lk 6:45).

PSALM 118-5 (119)

"Dispose my heart to follow Your statutes and to flee selfish gain"

A certain young woman was not in favor of the monk, Fr. Mina the Solitary (St. Pope Kyrillos VI), ascending to the See of St. Mark. She did not know Fr. Mina, but preferred another monk she did know. They were upset that the other monk was not chosen for the position of Patriarch. She remained unaccepting that St. Pope Kyrillos was head of the Church and decided not to see him.

One day, she was in downtown Alexandria shopping. Afterwards, she went to the Cathedral of Saint Mark to pray and receive a blessing before returning home. That was her usual habit. She found a priest praying Vespers covering his head with a white shawl. She stood transfixed, following his prayers, and her tears began flowing freely though she tried to hold them back.

When the priest was censing the church, he stopped, turned, and tapped her on the head with his Cross. He held her head between his hands and prayed. Afterwards, he asked her, "Why are you avoiding me? Tell your father, God willing, he should attend church tomorrow with the whole family to pray Matins, the Divine Liturgy, and partake of the Holy Communion." She was stunned and could not utter a single word.

Who was this person talking about her family without having any prior acquaintance? She burst into tears. As she was leaving, she asked the man responsible for baking the holy bread who this priest was. He answered that he was Pope Kyrillos! She was shocked by both his meekness and sanctity. She knew then that he was truly a man chosen by God.

On the Essence of Humility

St. Isaac the Syrian calls humility the "raiment" of the Godhead, Who "emptied himself, taking the form of a servant" (Php 2:7). St. Paul tells us that humility is the disposition and character of Christ's interior life, of which we must imitate. "Let this mind be in you which was also in Christ Jesus..." (Php 2:5). Since pride went before the Fall, of both Satan and man, there is in our nature a stubborn resistance to know ourselves as we truly are. The seduction of becoming gods apart from God is like a continual virus assaulting our nature.

It is curious that the disciples themselves, who after years of intimate discipleship to the Lord Jesus, continued to be plagued by this sin. On the eve of Christ's Passion, having mystically partaken of the Lord's Body and Blood, immediately after St. Luke comments, "Now there was also a dispute among them, as to which of them should be considered the greatest" (Lk 22:24). How dangerous and delicate religious life is! Again, St. Isaac the Syrian reminds us that every work, including the sublime apostleship of the twelve, is in vain without humility, for "Pride is hateful before God" (Sir 10:7).

The essence of humility, then, is truth and self-knowledge, to know what is rightly mine and what is God's. What properly belongs to me is nothingness and non-existence. I only exist because God called me into existence, my "being" is dependent on Him. I could do nothing to emerge from nothingness and I could do nothing to prevent my return to nothingness apart from God. "And what do you have that you did not receive? Now if you did indeed receive it, why do you boast as if you had not received it?" (1 Co 4:7).

Even in my moral life, only evil belongs to me since "God is light and in Him is no darkness at all" (1 Jn 1:5). Likewise, all good comes from Him and is not properly mine. We cannot on our own bear any fruit, as Jesus said, "for without Me you can do nothing" (Jn 15:5).

PSALM 118-6 (119)

"I will walk in complete freedom because I have sought Your commands"

When St. Pope Kyrillos VI stayed in Alexandria, St. Mark's Cathedral often organized trips to St. Mina's Monastery in Mariut. The Saint would often accompany these trips in his own car to visit the monastery and pray the Divine Liturgy there. The people used to gather around the Pope's car until he left and only then would they get on the bus to head toward the monastery.

On one of those trips, while a group of people were standing around the Pope's car, he turned to them and said, "Go and get on the bus!" However, they stayed and after some time he repeated the same words. They still chose to remain next to his car. The situation repeated itself a few times and when his car started moving they rushed toward the bus, but it had already left!

The private photographer of the Pope saw them and managed to get them onto a small microbus to take them to the monastery. On the way, the group was chanting praises for St. Mina. Since the microbus was smaller and faster, they caught up to the bus and passed it.

Along the way they saw a handsome young man waving for the microbus to stop. When they stopped he said to them, "You are chanting hymns, good for you!" They invited him in but he declined so they continued. They did not know where he came from or where he was going, but when they looked back wondering who this young man was that knew about their hymns, they no longer saw him.

After the Divine Liturgy, St. Pope Kyrillos started reprimanding them, "You should have listened to me and taken the bus instead of causing all this trouble! Who did you see on your way?" They told him they saw the bus and even passed it. He asked, "Who else did you see?" That was when they remembered the nice looking young man on the road who waved them down. The Saint said to them, "I sent you St. Mina!"

On the Virtue of Humility

A Croatian monk was on a tram and while getting off, because of the crowds, he involuntarily bumped into a youth. Furious, the youth slapped the monk on his face. Smiling gently, the monk said, "Please do the other side now. I should look awfully silly going about with only one red cheek." The youth was so embarrassed that, in the middle of the crowd, he got on his knees and asked forgiveness. The monk embraced him and said, "Nothing at all! Nothing at all! All forgotten now."

If pride goes before the fall, then humility goes before glory (Pr 15:33). One measure of humility is more valuable than multitudes of visions and revelations. Like a river, the flow of divine grace moves downward into a lowly heart. God dwells in the high and holy place but abides with the contrite and lowly (Is 57:15).

We should be grateful to anyone who helps keep us humble. Even if they had wicked intentions to humiliate us, if we are willing, we can use it to acquire humility. If this is too much to bear, then we can begin by giving thanks to God for everything and at all times, since acknowledging God as the giver of every good gift is an exercise in humility.

In the spiritual life, we are often perplexed why, after so much prayer and ascetical practices, we still fall into certain sins. Because pride and self-righteousness are so detrimental to our salvation, God will often permit the soul to fall into sins of the senses, in order to humble us, and safeguard us against the judgement and condemnation of our neighbor. This is the goodness of God who uses the manure of our sins as fertilizer for the increase in humility. Our sins, as one father commented, become a sledgehammer against Satan and against pride. The remembrance of death is the best teacher of truth. By it we learn the illusory nature of all that is vain and how to detach ourselves from it.

PSALM 118-7 (119)

"I remembered Your name, O Lord, in the night, and kept Your law"

A certain man was born in Shoubra in 1957, and when he was three years old, he contracted diphtheria which was very dangerous at that time. A well-known physician took his case and told the parents to bring him back for a follow-up two weeks after completing the treatment in order to avoid further complications. However, after two weeks the boy seemed to fully recover and the parents chose not to bring him back to the specialist. Fifteen days later, he became semi-paralyzed on the right side of his body. His condition continued to worsen and he soon lost the ability to swallow.

None of the treatments seemed to work. The father was devastated, until one day a merchant from Upper Egypt who was doing business with him asked him why he was so depressed. After the father related what was happening, the man told him, "Stop going to these earthly doctors. Go to Pope Kyrillos the spiritual doctor." He persuaded the parents to take the boy to see St. Pope Kyrillos VI the next morning to take his blessing.

The very next morning, the father covered the boy with a light sheet and took him to St. Mark's Church in Clot Bey. They arrived while Pope Kyrillos was censing the Altar. The father walked directly in front of the Saint, although several deacons tried to stop him. St. Pope Kyrillos asked him to come closer and uncover the boy's head. He laid his blessed hand on the boy's head and said a lengthy prayer. Then he told the father, "You can go now, the Lord will heal your son." At the end of the service they took Holy Communion and for the first time in three months he was able to swallow. By the grace of God and through the prayers of the Saint, the boy completely recovered.

On Difficulties in Prayer

If we are serious about maintaining a personal prayer life, we should be prepared to encounter all sorts of obstacles and setbacks. The first among them is time. If we view our life through the lens of faith and the perspective of eternity, the most important activity of our day is prayer. What should distinguish us as Christians is the supernatural life within us. That is our value to the world and the true aid to my neighbor. Otherwise at best, I am just a good social worker or philanthropist. Our contact with God, as poor as it may seem from our assessment, is our greatest service to others.

Aridity, or dryness, in prayer poses another perceived threat to the quality of our prayer. The only conditions required for pure prayer are faith and a desire to please God. God's proximity to us in prayer is not confirmed by feelings or even supernatural experiences. On the contrary, our prayer is more selfless, more valuable and more heroic when it is not supported by our feelings and emotions. God, who is pure self-gift, sees in us our own self-gift to Him, when it seems we get nothing from prayer.

As we get older, taking on more responsibilities, perhaps acquiring a certain stature among others, we risk approaching God without a childlike disposition. "Assuredly, I say to you, unless you are converted and become as little children, you will by no means enter the kingdom of heaven" (Mt 18:3). When Jesus taught us the Lord's Prayer, He used the word "Abba" (Mt 6:9), an affectionate term typically used by children to address their father. The attitude of a child not only establishes a filial conversation with God, but instills us with trust in the midst of our trials, and a secure home after sin (Lk 15:24).

Prayer is more about God's activity in us. The Holy Spirit intercedes for us "for we do not know how to pray as we should" (Ro 8:26). This should remove our anxiety about the quality of our prayer. It is enough for us to desire to be with God and to please Him.

PSALM 118-8 (119)

"I have reflected on my ways and resolved to follow Your precepts"

In 1963, a woman suffered from excruciating pain in the abdominal area along with a high fever. She saw many specialists throughout Cairo and Alexandria. They prescribed several types of medications but none of them helped. There were different medical opinions but her condition continued to worsen. Her whole body was swollen and she was unable to sleep from the severe pain. Her kidneys were also affected from all of the medication.

This continued for seven years until a large lump protruded from the abdominal area and an investigational surgery was scheduled. Before the surgery, her brother-in-law suggested that she visit St. Pope Kyrillos VI, who happened to be in Alexandria.

Despite the fact that she had never met the Pope before, as soon as she stood before him, he put his hand over her head and prayed. Before she had a chance to tell him about her ailments, he said, "Go home, my lady. There will not be an operation." She tried to explain her medical condition to him, but he would not let her speak. He insisted she go home and reiterated that surgery would not be necessary. He then blessed her with his Cross.

She returned home wondering, "How did His Holiness know what was wrong with me and my scheduled operation without me saying a word?" The specialists rechecked her and they were all astonished by the visible changes to her condition. They canceled the operation, stopped all medications, and allowed her to return to work. All the aches were gone and the lab tests came back normal. The tumor vanished without a trace and she became completely healthy due to the prayers and blessings of St. Pope Kyrillos VI.

On Guarding the Tongue

Temperance is the virtue of moderation. It is often associated with the practice of fasting which moderates gluttony. But it equally applies to other passions and its objective is to produce modesty and sobriety in our words and actions. The gift of speech is unique to man, given to him to praise God and enjoy fellowship with one another, not through instinct like animals, but in intimate understanding and communication.

Through our speech, the Word of God is preached and heard, enabling it to penetrate deep into human hearts. By it, we comfort and console one another through life's pains and difficulties. But the tongue, St. James says, is "a little member and boasts great things...an unruly evil, full of deadly poison. With it we bless our God and Father, and with it we curse men, who have been made in the similitude of God. Out of the same mouth proceed blessing and cursing" (Jas 3:5,8-10). Such effect does the tongue have on building up and destroying that it becomes a unique focus of the soul's judgment. "For by your words you will be justified, and by your words you will be condemned" (Mt 12:37).

The saints likened gossip and slander to the deeds of a murderer. Moreover, temperance applies to the avoidance of useless and superficial conversations, including coarse joking. "But I say to you that for every idle word men may speak, they will give account of it in the day of judgment" (Mt 12:36).

The tongue is a sacrament of the heart; it is meant to "impart grace to those who hear" (Eph 4:29). The Lord said, "For out of the abundance of the heart the mouth speaks" (Lk 6:45). Not only is speech a reflection of the good or evil in one's heart, but these words could also be understood in another sense. Because of the abundance of the heart, the tongue speaks little as the soul prefers to converse with God in the silence of the heart. But when the heart is empty, the tongue is full of useless talkativeness.

PSALM 118-9 (119)

"Sweet are You, O Lord, and what You do is good"

A certain man went with his family to take the blessing of St. Pope Kyrillos VI at St. Mark's Cathedral in Alexandria but they were unable to meet him. They remained on the ground floor with many other visitors and were shouting, "Long live the Pope!" and requesting his blessing. The Pope came out, blessed them with the sign of the Cross and with holy water.

His daughter cried out, "The Virgin! The Virgin!" Those present were surprised and asked her, "Where?!" She answered, "There! By the Pope's side, with a white veil and her body is all light! Her face is like the sun!"

The family was returning home, but the girl kept asking them to return in order to see the Virgin Mary again. Nothing could convince the girl that it was unlikely to see the Virgin again. The next morning, the girl woke up unable to speak. The family spent the day in confusion and the following morning hurried back to see the Saint.

During the liturgical prayers, as the Pope passed by with the censer, her mother presented the girl to the Pope and asked him to place the Cross on her head. But the Pope looked at her harshly and said, "Stay in your place, girl!" The girl turned to her mother and said, "Why did the Pope do this?" So, the Pope bent down to her and said, "So, now you are speaking?"

The mother was puzzled by the exchange and said to the Pope, "She saw the Virgin Mary by your side." The Pope asked, "When?" She replied, "Yesterday, Your Holiness." But the Saint, enlightened by the Holy Spirit, asked the girl, "Is that correct?" The girl answered, "No, Your Holiness, it was the day before yesterday!" And the Pope confirmed, "You are right!"

On the Spiritual Maternity of the Theotokos

Mothers give birth to persons, not natures. The mystery of the Virgin's motherhood is steeped in the mystery of the Incarnation; God has become man, fully God and fully man, without sin, but He is one Person. St. Mary is the Theotokos, the Mother of God. Elizabeth, naturally and spontaneously, asks how it is possible to be so highly honored, "That the Mother of my Lord should come to me?" Any attempt in Christian history to diminish or soften the role of the Virgin Mary as Theotokos was met with resistance. The Virgin Mary is perpetually the Mother of God.

The maternity of the Theotokos is not relegated to speculative or dogmatic theology, but has a concrete relation to spiritual life. If God has given us His Only-Begotten Son for our redemption, and the Holy Spirit for our sanctification, He has also given us a Mother, full of tender compassion, encouragement and bold intercession for us before God. "Woman, behold your son" (Jn 19:26).

In giving birth to her Son, she brought forth for us our true life; she feels bound to protect that life in us. The intense love she feels for her Son, she directs to us as well. As God prepared her to be the perfect Mother of the Word, He likewise prepared her to be the perfect Mother for us.

We will never love the Virgin Mary more than her Son. But we should enter into the tenderness of that love between Mother and Son, learning from her how to love Christ, and also learning from Christ how to love His mother. Christ is "of the Holy Spirit and of the Virgin Mary" (*Nicene Creed*). St. Mary is the greatest saint, the best human imitation of her Son. But Christ's own human soul also resembles His mother.

She is the mother acquainted with our sorrows, the helper in times of temptation, the intercessor of our repentance, comfort in our hopelessness, and the protectress of the Church. "O pure Virgin, overshadow your servant with your instant help...For you are a capable, compassionate, and helpful mother, the bearer of the Fountain of Life, my King and my God, Jesus Christ, my hope" (*Litany of the 12th Hour*).

PSALM 118-10 (119)

"May my heart be blameless toward Your decrees, so I may not be put to shame"

A young man went to take the blessing of St. Pope Kyrillos VI who was visiting the Monastery of St. Mary in Assiut. There was such a large crowd that he could not reach him to take the blessing of kissing his hand carrying the Cross. He thought that if he could just touch his shawl, he would receive the same blessings as the others. Sure enough, though the crowd was dense, he managed to touch the shawl of the Saint.

On his way back, he started having some doubts as to whether he had really received a blessing since he did not kiss the Saint's hand and the Cross. So, he turned around, went back, and struggled through all the crowd to reach the Pope. Just before kissing his hand with the Cross, the Saint said to him, "Wasn't the other blessing enough?" At that moment, he came to realize the great sanctity in St. Pope Kyrillos VI.

On Simplicity

"At that time Jesus answered and said, "I thank You, Father, Lord of heaven and earth, that You have hidden these things from the wise and prudent and have revealed them to babes" (Mt 11:25). In a profound contradiction, the uncovering of the mystery of salvation and holiness has uniquely become the possession of the child-like, while the wise and learned have become confounded in themselves. "He catches the wise in their own craftiness" (1 Co 3:19). Simplicity is not naïveté or ignorance. It is actually one of the most important divine attributes of God. God is not composite, or composed of parts, He is pure simple being. Nor are His attributes (mercy, justice, will) different parts in conflict with one another. There is no duplicity in God, He is simple. Likewise, the simple person is single in focus, not divided, uncomplicated, not duplicitous.

Simplicity is purity of intention. "If your eye is single your whole body shall be full of light" (Mt 6:22). The simple person's focus is not divided, it is wholly on God. Jesus is the exemplar of simplicity. "My food is to do the will of Him who sent Me, and to finish His work" (Jn 4:34). The Lord was never conflicted about His mission, nor hindered by Satan's temptations, nor did He become fainthearted in the face of suffering. Rather, because of "the joy that was set before Him (He) endured the Cross, despising the shame..." (Heb 12:2).

Simplicity, then, is the virtue by which, through the aid of divine grace, we begin to unify and purify our soul, directed to one end—God. The soul becomes attentive to any secondary intentions, sins, distractions, and deviations that creep in and derail it. Man is complex when he serves more than one master. Everything is motivated by love and is directed to love. The simple person likewise guards against a preoccupation with the self. We must not be overly rigorous, exacting, and fussy with ourselves. The saints who exhibited simplicity displayed freedom in their actions, lightness, and spontaneity before God, trusting in the singleness of their love for Him.

PSALM 118-11 (119)

"My eyes fail, looking for Your word, and I cry out, 'When will You comfort me?'"

A certain man's daughter and her husband were living in El Arish (North Sinai) with their two little daughters. In June 1967, Israel occupied the whole area and the parents did not hear from them for two and a half years, causing them great distress and worry. They continued in steadfast prayers asking for the intercessions of the saints.

His other daughter went to St. Mark's Cathedral to take the blessing of St. Pope Kyrillos VI. She asked the Saint to pray for her sister and family who were still in El Arish. The Saint asked, "Isn't your sister (...) and her husband (...) and their daughters (... and...)? They are all well and coming soon. Do not worry!" She was puzzled as the Pope listed all their names although he did not know any of them.

When she returned home and told her mother what happened, the mother rebuked her, thinking she was joking. But fifteen days later, the daughter arrived from El Arish with her husband and their two daughters. And so the Saint's prophecy came true.

On Living the Eucharist - Sacrament and Word

The Eucharist is the sacrament of sanctification and union with God. It is both a divine grace and an illumination into the complete mystery of Christian life. It permeates us fully and yet extends us to uncover new grace. Seven principles of a Eucharistic life are arrayed every time the community gathers to break bread: sacrament, word, paschal mystery, trinity, church, thanksgiving (praise), and petition.

The Eucharist reveals the sacramentality of creation. The word "sacrament" usually expresses the outward sign or symbol, while the word "mystery" speaks to the hidden but real divine presence. We can speak of Jesus as the Sacrament of the Father in that the Incarnation is the visible reality of God in the flesh, who is "the image of the invisible God" (Col 1:15). God created the world as a sacrament of His presence. Because it comes from His creative love it is "very good" (Ge 1:31). The Eucharist is the sacrament par excellence as it makes present the perfect love of God and the power of Christ's death and resurrection abiding in us unto eternal life. It therefore instructs us and guides us to discover God's presence which "is present in all places and fills all things" (*Litany of the Third Hour of the Coptic Agpeya*).

Before the Eucharist is taken under the appearance of bread and wine, we receive the inspired written word by the Holy Spirit. God speaks to us in the biblical word, immersing us in His language and the language of His Kingdom. Little by little, we exchange the words and language of the world for the heavenly word. His word becomes our word, His thoughts become our thoughts, His deeds become our deeds, so that we can truly be the salt of the earth and the light of the world. Each baptized Christian has an obligation to speak the language of God to others, to sanctify the world, and it is there in the Eucharist where we are inducted into God's family and service.

PSALM 118-12 (119)

"I am Yours; save me"

In 1967, a certain couple's two-year-old son developed a fever of 39 degrees Celsius (over 102 degrees Fahrenheit) that could not be lowered. After many tests, the doctors diagnosed it as rheumatic fever. Nothing could be done other than biweekly injections of penicillin and complete bed rest. This was very difficult because he was a very active toddler who loved playing with his four-year-old sister. They were told that the injections would have to continue for several years so that his heart would not be affected.

They implored the Lord to help them through this difficult time. A family member bought them tickets to visit St. Mina's Monastery in Mariut and ask for St. Pope Kyrillos' prayers. At first they thought the trip would be too difficult on their son, but finally agreed to go.

As soon as they arrived, the Pope greeted them and the boy immediately exclaimed, "I am sick!" The Saint looked at him with deep paternal love and compassion and put his Cross on his head and prayed. Then he said, "It is finished, you are healed."

After a few days they went to the doctor for a routine visit. To their great surprise, the boy completely recovered. The doctor, however, could not explain why.

On Living the Eucharist - the Paschal Mystery

"[U]nless a grain of wheat falls into the ground and dies, it remains alone; but if it dies, it produces much grain" (Jn 12:24). The grain of wheat is the mystery of Christ's death and resurrection. This transformation of the grain of wheat also points to the mystery of the Eucharist, the Bread of Life. Christ offered Himself in the Bread and Wine before the unfolding of the events on Holy Friday. He wants to assure us that He is total self-gift, nothing is taken from Him that He has not already willingly and lovingly offered.

"Do this in remembrance of Me" (Lk 22:19). These words at the breaking of the Bread come after Jesus washed the feet of the disciples. At that time He said to them, "For I have given you an example, that you should do as I have done to you" (Jn 13:15). What links these two events is the mystery of Christ's love which He expects all who believe in Him to imitate. The two commands to "do" what the Lord did in the breaking of the Bread and the washing of the feet are not related to future ritual ceremonies, but to a way of life for the disciple. They both point to the dying to the self, in order to live for others. Every time we partake of the Eucharist, we enter into the Lord's Death and Resurrection; we receive His life and His capacity to offer ourselves with Him.

As Christ broke the Bread, signifying His sacrificial offering for the life of the world, we are also called to be broken and distributed, "carrying about in the body the dying of the Lord Jesus, that the life of Jesus also may be manifested in our body" (2 Co 4:10). The Eucharist is the extreme presentation of the Lord's humility. He condescends in His divinity to put on humanity, and further condescends to become bread and wine. In doing so, He has become utterly vulnerable and approachable. And then St. Paul's words echo in our hearts, "Let this mind be in you which was also in Christ Jesus" (Php 2:5).

PSALM 118-13 (119)

"Through Your commandments I achieve wisdom; therefore I hate every way of unrighteousness"

In 1968, an accountant was facing problems at his work with a new accounting system which created lots of confusion. It needed lots of hard work and effort in order to apply it in a satisfactory manner. Sometimes he worked until 2:00 am from home. On August 28, 1968, he went to St. Mark's Cathedral in Cairo, toward the very end of the Divine Liturgy. He was carrying file folders to do more work at home.

Before he reached the inside of the door of the church, he saw a crowd and assumed that the Pope was distributing the blessed bread (*antidoron*) to the congregation. He stood in line waiting for his turn. When the Pope saw him, he motioned for him to come closer although he was nearly at the end of the line. He went to His Holiness who then asked him, "Why do you stay late at work?" He started to answer, "Your Holiness...," but without letting him finish, he continued, "Come here, I know. Lower your head." So the Saint put the man's head on his knees and placed the Cross on his head. He took the folders and put them on a chair next to him and kept praying. He also put the Cross inside the folders and prayed saying, "Take them [the folders] my son, may God help you and guide you, and make things easy for you. Count on the blessings of Christ."

He immediately felt that the heavy burden of the tiring hours he spent for the last few months had been taken away. He was greatly comforted and full of inner joy.

He left the church, and all the way to work, he could clearly hear a voice saying, "Why confuse yourself going in circles? You can simply do...," and the voice explained to him the best system to follow. He arrived at his office and locked himself in a room and started applying what he heard. Within three hours, he covered almost the entire year's work in the most ideal method. He showed the results to his superiors at work, and they were impressed and very pleased with him.

On Living the Eucharist - the Trinity and the Church

At the center of the eucharistic liturgy is the revelation and worship of the Holy Trinity. Standing at the door of the Sanctuary and holding up the eucharistic gifts, the priest begins the celebration with the words, "Glory and honor, honor and glory be to the all-Holy Trinity, the Father, the Son and the Holy Spirit." After processing the gifts around the Altar and blessing them, the people chant, "Glory to the Father and the Son and the Holy Spirit." And at the end of the Liturgy, just before Holy Communion is distributed, the priest prays inaudibly, "For at all times, all glory and all honor and all worship are due to the Holy Trinity, the Father, and the Son and the Holy Spirit..."

God is glorified when He is manifested, known, loved, and worshiped. The Eucharist is the celebration and proclamation of God's glory as it demonstrates the Trinity's creative, redemptive, and salvific works "for the life of the world" (Jn 6:51). It perpetuates and extends His glory, because it is the Good News of our liberation from sin and death, and our incorporation in God's eternal family. The Eucharist is an invitation to come "inside" the bosom of the Trinity: "Go out quickly into the streets and lanes of the city, and bring in here the poor and the maimed and the lame and the blind...Go out into the highways and hedges, and compel them to come in, that My house may be filled" (Lk 14:21,23).

The Church is the assembly called into a covenant relationship with God. "He made us unto Himself an assembled people, and sanctified us by Your Holy Spirit" (*Divine Liturgy of St. Basil*). We are called out of our individuality into fellowship and communion with one another. The Eucharist actualizes a continuous process of unity at the level of the local parish, diocese, universal church, and the heavenly church, "that we may become one body and one spirit, and may have a share and inheritance with all the saints who have pleased You since the beginning" (*Divine Liturgy of St. Basil*).

The eucharistic prayers are said in the plural ("we," "our," "us"), not in the singular. The priest who stands representing the whole community offers saying, "We offer unto You Your gifts from what is Yours..." By transcending individuality, our unity removes all envy, competition, and malice.

PSALM 118-14 (119)

"I have been very greatly afflicted, O Lord, let me live according to Your word"

When he was born in 1954, a certain man suffered from infantile paralysis in both legs. In 1960 when St. Pope Kyrillos VI visited El Menoufia, he was six years old and still not able to walk at all. During the Saint's stay in El Menoufia, the boy was carried on a cot to him in the same manner the paralytic was carried by his four friends in the time of Jesus. They pushed their way through the crowd to get to the Saint.

As soon as the Pope noticed them, he said, "Bring me the chanter's son so I can pray for him." He said this although he did not know them and no one had the chance to tell him anything.

When the Pope finished his prayer, both legs stretched out and almost all of the symptoms of the disease vanished. He was able to walk on his own with only a very mild symptom remaining in the right leg.

On Living the Eucharist - Thanksgiving and Petition

The Eucharist is a thanksgiving "for everything, concerning everything, and in everything" (*Thanksgiving Prayer*). Gratitude is the primordial posture of man before God, in acknowledgement that he has received his very "being" from Him, and that "every good gift and every perfect gift is from above, and comes down from the Father of lights" (Jas 1:17). In the eucharistic liturgy, man recounts the goodness of God in all His works and promises, and in return offers back to God his very life. The water mixed with the wine is the life of man, who is united to God both in His sacrifice and in His life.

Gratitude is the door to praise. One cannot praise God from the heart if he is not filled with awe and wonder at God's goodness. In the Eucharist, we find pleasure in praising God above all our self-interests and requests for temporal goods: "We praise You...we give thanks to You for Your great glory!" (*The Gloria*) Through gratitude, man discovers his vocation, for he alone has the unique gift to praise God in thanksgiving.

Petition and intercession are expressions of our love for one another and for the creation. We ask within our rights as true children of God, full of confidence and boldness: "...with firm hope, we may dare with boldness, without fear, to pray to You..." (*Annual Fraction, Divine Liturgy of St. Basil*). The Eucharist is a pedagogy of love. Incorporated into the mystery of God's creative, redemptive, and salvific plan, our hearts spontaneously cry out for the goodness of God to be poured out for the salvation of the world, the peace of the Church, the poor and miserable, the animals and elements, and for the souls of the departed. A eucharistic life is one of growing in compassion and sensitivity to the needs of others, along with a fervent desire for perfect unity.

PSALM 118-15 (119)

"Sustain me according to Your promise, and I will live; do not delude me in my hope"

A certain man suffered from many diseases that affected him psychologically. He was examined and treated by many doctors, but it was all in vain. Some advised him to see St. Pope Kyrillos VI, but because of his lack of faith, he was hesitant to go.

When he became desperate, he decided to visit the Pope who was at St. Mina's Monastery in Mariut at that time. He asked the Saint to pray for him who then covered him with the sacred vestment he was wearing during Liturgy and prayed. However, he did not get better and turned to the Pope and said, "I am not leaving this place till I recover!"

The Saint looked at him with compassion and asked him to sit down on a chair and prayed for him again. The Pope then whispered in his ear, "Here is St. Mina, he came especially for you!" The man said that he immediately felt as if electricity was going through his body. When the Saint finished praying, he felt that all his sickness left him, and he shouted, "I recovered Your Holiness, I recovered!"

On Judgment and Condemnation

Judgment always begins with some form of comparison. From a young age we are taught to always make comparisons with others as it relates to our grades, athletics, and even at church. These comparisons then make their way as moral judgments, "that person is worse than me!" Self-love is the root of judgement. When I judge another, I make myself better than them, feeding my self-love. It also grants me a sort of pass in not having to extend Christian charity to them - "He is just an alcoholic bum so I'm not giving him anything!"

St. Dorotheos of Gaza describes a three-fold progression: slander, judgment, and condemnation. To slander is to say, "this person has stolen." With judgement we go further and say, "this person is a thief." And in condemning the person, we conclude, "there is no salvation for him!" St. John Climacus warns us that our judgment is worse than the sin the person committed. The sinner may be humbled and repent, he says, but judgment makes us like the Devil.

Judgment is a lack of self-knowledge. Someone was asked, what is the most difficult thing for him? He replied: "To know oneself." "And what is easiest?" "To see the shortcomings of our neighbors." If we know ourselves well, focusing on our own sins and repentance, even when confronted with the sin of my brother, my heart will cry out, "Alas! Him today, me tomorrow!" Judgment is also a sign that we lack compassion. While we do not dismiss that an act someone committed is objectively wrong, we are still called to go beyond the act and find compassion for the person who, in some sense, is also a victim. Elder Paisios of Mount Athos gave the example of two friends walking along a path when someone jumps out from behind a bush and pounces on one of them, beating him up. Would it not be totally unreasonable and unjust, he asked, to blame that friend? But this is what we do when we condemn someone who was pounced on by Satan. Again, St. Dorotheos says that only God knows the situation of each person, their strength, and environment. Only God can justify or condemn. "Judge not, and you shall not be judged" (Lk 6:37).

PSALM 118-16 (119)

"I am Your servant; grant me discernment so that I may understand Your statutes"

A certain man was living with his brother and sister-in-law, who started to get annoyed by his stay. He was still a student and did not have the financial means to live on his own. But one day, his brother asked him to look for another place to live. The young man was deeply hurt and felt like everything was dark in his life. The next day was a Friday and he left early without breakfast and went to the church. While he was at the tram station, his keys fell and landed about two meters away from him. Bending to pick them up, he found a five piaster coin which he took and went to a nearby food stand. He ate fava beans and falafel sandwiches with three piasters and used two piasters as fare to and from the Patriarchate.

At the Patriarchate, he went to see St. Pope Kyrillos VI. He looked at him intensely and said, "What happened, my son? What is wrong?" He answered, "It seems God has forgotten me." The Saint said, "No, He has not, it is you who has forgotten! Didn't He just feed you beans and falafel? How then can He forget you?" The young man could not say a word. Truly, he had forgotten that when he thought everyone had abandoned him, the Lord never did. He left the Saint glorifying God and thanking him for his many favors. He went back to his brother's place full of consolation and peace. Indeed, there was even a great change in his brother who received him with a warm welcome.

On Christian Freedom

Freedom is a unique gift from God to man. This gift is given to man so that he might choose and work toward his union with God by loving Him. The effect of sin and death enslaved man. In the divine plan, the Son of God liberated us from the bonds of our enslavement, and obtained for us the divine sonship through the Holy Spirit. This is what St. Paul calls, "the liberty by which Christ has made us free" (Ga 5:1).

Today, the concept of freedom implies the right to act on any impulse or desire. Whereas, the liberty of the children of God is the freedom to not have to act on every impulse or desire, in order to pursue his own perfection. The freedom of a professional musician is not the ability to choose between right and wrong musical notes; it is the mastery by which they have the liberty to play the music perfectly, without striking any bad notes.

That is why Christian freedom necessitates obedience to God and His will, Who is the source and means of our ability to fulfill our vocation, and to obtain our greatest good, namely union with God and eternal happiness. It would be absurd to assert that God is a limitation to freedom when freedom is precisely His gift to us. Jesus is the perfect model of freedom who was "obedient even unto death" (Php 2:8) in order to fulfill the will of the Father. The Mother of God, St. Mary, called herself "the handmaiden of the Lord" (Lk 1:38) confirming that perfect submission to God is a "slavery of love" giving freedom its perfect meaning.

Our freedom in Christ finds its strength in our being elevated to divine sonship and friendship with God. "No longer do I call you servants...but I have called you friends" (Jn 15:15). His friendship frees us from responding to God out of fear of punishment. Our surrender to Him is done out of a joyful obedience. Our clinging to Him, despite our weaknesses and falls, is the pledge of our freedom that works in us now, until our filiation is consummated in full. "Therefore if the Son makes you free, you shall be free indeed" (Jn 8:36).

PSALM 118-17 (119)

"Streams of tears flow from my eyes because Your law is disregarded"

One day, a woman was sitting on the beach, and when she tried to stand up, she could not. They took her to a doctor who said that she was suffering from a slipped disc and that she needed surgery. After the surgery, she still could not walk, so she was sent overseas for further treatment, but still there was no improvement. After all the money spent, she had to wear an iron belt around her waist and legs; she wore it for seven years.

Some of her relatives visited her one day and mentioned they were going to visit St. Pope Kyrillos VI. She wept and asked them to tell the Saint about her condition and to ask him to pray for her. When they told the Pope her story, he gave them a piece of cotton anointed with holy oil and a piece of a string. The Saint prayed on both. The sick lady was anointed with the oil and tied the string around her waist, according to the instructions given by the Saint, and went to sleep. In the morning, she woke up calling her relatives to untie the iron belt that was hurting her and limiting her movement. When they untied her, she started walking in the room.

On Conversion

In today's language, conversion usually means a change in religion or from unbelief to faith. But conversion is a dynamic element in Christian spirituality that is best described as transformation. "Do not be conformed to this world but be transformed by the renewal of your mind" (Ro 12:2). The basis of ongoing conversion is the call to a higher degree of the interior life of perfection. It is a pull in the spiritual life that eradicates faintheartedness and worldly accommodations that disrupt its progress. Conversion is an attitude, a strong determination for holiness for the sake of pleasing God.

Conversion touches every aspect of spiritual life. It is a continuum of degrees in fervor and love for God. It can also be viewed as a convergence, a gathering of all our scattered priorities, affections, and acts, toward a single goal and end. Signs of a life of conversion include a greater conformity to God's will, a stronger distaste for sin, a more fervent desire for God's glory, and the acceptance of suffering and the Cross. What is required of us is greater desire, hunger, and longing. The execution of those desires is given by grace. That is why conversion also requires more heroic patience, endurance, and the rejection of all forms of discouragement.

God's will is for us all to be saints. "For this is the will of God, your sanctification" (1 Th 4:3). In the beginning stage of the spiritual life, the will of God is accepted with difficulty and the Cross is felt to be heavy. In the second stage, we seek God with a healthy devotion and find more joy in accepting the Cross. Among the perfect, there is no joy outside of God's will and the Cross is sought for the sole purpose of proving our love to Christ. In the Gospel, Jesus sensed those whose hearts were open to an encounter with Him. For many, there was an eruption of new life from a single contact with the Lord. Likewise, we must always seek the encounter whether in prayer, spiritual reading, and especially in the Holy Eucharist. In those moments, ask the Lord for the grace of conversion, for a new and stable disposition to become holy because it is His desire that we become so.

PSALM 118-18 (119)

"I am afflicted by anguish and distress, but Your precepts are my delight"

A certain man was diagnosed with coronary heart disease and after consulting various physicians, they all agreed he needed complete rest for at least one month and to remain on a strict diet.

One day, he decided to partake of the Holy Communion and asked one of the priests for the absolution since he was not fasting the Advent Fast due to his strict diet. The priest refused to give him the absolution. St. Pope Kyrillos VI was there and inquired about the problem. When the Saint was told about his circumstances, he gave him absolution and Holy Communion.

After the Divine Liturgy, he went to the Pope's cell but did not find him there, so he sat down on one of the chairs and waited for him. When the Pope arrived he told him, "You are sitting on my chair" and patted him with his Cross. The man stood quickly but the Saint insisted that he remain seated. Interestingly, all the chairs were exactly alike and none were designated for the Pope.

Amazingly, while the man was initially waiting in the Pope's cell, the Saint was actually preparing breakfast for him. Afterwards he asked the man what was wrong with him and he told him the story of his heart disease. The Saint put his hand on his chest and prayed and said, "That is it, there is no more problem, you are now very well."

Indeed, he left the monastery a new person. He felt no sickness and had enough energy to walk up the stairs to his office on the ninth floor without any discomfort or exhaustion.

On the Holy Spirit and Unity

On the great day of Pentecost, the Lord inaugurated the reunification of all peoples. The sin of pride separated and divided those at Babel (Ge 11:5-9) and so God sent the Holy Spirit to restore unity and love. As mankind spiraled into disintegration by language, race, and social status, the Holy Spirit removed all such distinctions. But Jesus was clear that the unity God seeks among His people is not a false unity, but one built on the truth. "Do you think that I have come to bring peace to the earth? No, I tell you, but rather division!" (Lk 12:51).

Pentecost has also been called the birthday of the Church. St. Augustine said, "the world reconciled" is the Church. That is, the Church is "the pillar and foundation of the truth" (1 Ti 3:15) and, therefore, the cause of unity. The Church is not a social institution to do good in the world, as noble as that might be, but a confirmation and evidence that our end is a supernatural end, and our destiny is an eternal one. The Church is the icon of unity, where "there is neither Jew nor Greek, there is neither slave nor free, there is neither male nor female; for you are all one in Christ Jesus" (Ga 3:28). Christ has chosen to live and act by and through His Church. It is His own construction, "I will build My Church" (Mt 16:18). In the Christian Creed, the Church is an object of faith: "We believe in One God, Father Almighty...We believe in one Lord Jesus Christ...we believe in the Holy Spirit...and in One, Holy, Catholic, and Apostolic Church." It is not something incidental or secondary.

But is not the Church on the verge of destruction from persecutions, internal corruption and scandals, and the external pressures of deviant immorality, relativism, and atheism? As the Fathers and saints have so often commented, many have assailed the Church but they have perished and the Church remains. For the Lord promised and He is her keeper, "the gates of Hades shall not prevail against it" (Mt 16:18).

PSALM 118-19 (119)

"Yet You, O Lord, are near, and all Your precepts are true"

A certain priest went with eighteen of his fellow priests to visit St. Pope Kyrillos VI at the Monastery of St. Mina. At that time he was the General Vicar for the Patriarchate and needed to discuss some church matters with the Pope.

In those early days, the road to the monastery was not paved and visitors had to follow a path in the desert guided by landmarks on both sides. On their way, they missed the marks and found themselves lost in the middle of a vast desert. There was nobody to ask how to get back on the road even if they wanted to return back.

Suddenly, a Bedouin appeared asking them, "Do you want to go to St. Mina's Monastery?" They were surprised and, of course, answered in the affirmative. With total simplicity, he sat in the car and began to direct the driver until they reached the monastery. Their hearts were full of praise and gratitude to the Lord Jesus Christ who did not abandon them in the great desert.

They found St. Pope Kyrillos VI waiting for them at the monastery gate. He asked in a fatherly and compassionate way, "What is the matter, my son? Did you lose your way?" The priest replied, "We lost the way, but God sent us a Bedouin who led us until we arrived."

The Saint, with an angelic smile on his face, asked, "Where is he?" They went looking for the man but there was no trace of him. When they went back to the Pope, he smiled pleasantly and said, "My son, I sent you St. Mina when you lost your way!"

On the Remembrance of God

One of the greatest sins of the nation of Israel in the Old Testament is that of forgetfulness. Repeatedly, the cycles of sin, of idolatry and immorality, can all be traced back to forgetfulness. "Because you have forgotten the God of your salvation" (Is 17:10). Throughout the Holy Week services, the prophecies come back to this theme over and over again. Jesus uses the Parable of the Wicked Tenants and delivers a blow to the heart of the chosen race: "Therefore I say to you, the kingdom of

God will be taken from you and given to a nation bearing the fruits of it" (Mt 21:43).

The disciples likewise suffered the fate of forgetfulness. Right after the Feeding of the Multitudes (Mk 6:30-42), Jesus sends them across the Sea of Galilee to Bethsaida while he dismisses the multitude and spends time in prayer. Caught in a storm, Jesus comes to them walking on the water. He enters their boat, and calms both the sea and their troubled hearts. But St. Mark says something peculiar, "And they were greatly amazed in themselves beyond measure, and marveled. For they had not understood about the loaves, because their heart was hardened." The hardness of their heart was due to their forgetfulness and the lack of care given to ponder, reflect, consider, and remember the works of God.

The same warning should arouse us to be watchful. Regular participation in the divine services, especially the Eucharist, drives away forgetfulness. "For every time you shall eat of this bread and drink of this cup, you proclaim My Death, confess My Resurrection and remember Me till I come" (*Divine Liturgy of St. Basil*). The seasons of fasting in the Church also have as a simple objective the remembrance of God. When I fast, I remember "why" I am fasting. Every moment of our day can be filled with the remembrance of God through the Jesus Prayer or a simple glance at Him. Elder Paisios of Mount Athos warned us not to be like a child who is so absorbed in his toys that he is unaware of his father's caresses.

PSALM 118-20 (119)

"See my suffering and deliver me, for I have not forgotten Your law"

A certain lady was suffering from a serious illness and every kind of treatment failed. Her health deteriorated to the point that she was suffering from intolerable pain and was screaming day and night because of it. Since medicine did not help her, the people close to her began praying for her eternal rest. Some suggested that she go seek the help of St. Pope Kyrillos VI, to which her husband responded with sarcasm.

After repeated requests, they went to the Pope at St. Mark's Cathedral in Cairo. The Saint prayed for the eternal rest of the sick lady, which made the husband very angry. He left saying some harsh words about the Pope. The Saint's prayers were answered and the lady departed the next day to Paradise.

The next day, the husband returned to St. Pope Kyrillos, feeling ashamed and wanting to apologize. The Saint, in his usual fatherly kindness, immediately forgave him and asked God to give the man comfort in the face of what he was experiencing. He said to him, "My son, I saw her spirit ascending to heaven during the morning prayers." He then indicated the exact time that she passed away. He also assured the man that he completely forgave him for every word that he had said against him.

The husband left the room very surprised by the actions of the Pope, who knew every word the husband had uttered against him the previous day.

On the Suffering of Abandonment

There are two characteristics of one who truly loves: doing good for the other, and suffering for them. Since God could not suffer, He took our humanity and ascended upon the Cross in order to manifest His love for us to the end. The physical tortures and pain of the Passion of Christ were visible to His bystanders, but the depth of His interior suffering was hidden and unknown. While His physical tortures lasted but for a time, His soul was in sorrow from the beginning. He knew that

His love would be rejected by many, and that countless souls would despise their own salvation, choosing the way of destruction.

Apart from glimpses of His agony in the silence of the Garden in Gethsemane, we can glean from the prophecies of the Old Testament what was happening in the soul of the Savior. "But I am a worm, and not a man; a reproach of men, and scorn of the people" (Ps 21:6). It is an image of shame and abandonment. Even His own disciples would not be much support; in His greatest vulnerability, He would have to travel alone. "I have trodden the winepress alone, and from the peoples no one was with Me" (Is 63:3).

If we are to resemble Christ, following Him in all His steps from the Cross to the tomb and rising up with Him into glory, we must also travel at times in the way of abandonment. "My God, My God, why have You forsaken Me?" (Mt 27:46, Ps 21:1). This is the mysterious cry of Jesus from the Cross. How can we understand it? Was He reciting the Psalm to direct us to the fulfillment of the prophecies? Was He actually abandoned by the Father? Church teaching is clear that there was no possible separation between the Father and the Son. But we must not diminish the real love of Christ who voluntarily chose to enter all our pain and suffering in every possible way, except for sin. If God could become man, it was because He chose to do so. If He could suffer and die on the Cross, it was because He chose to do so. And if He voluntarily accepted to experience the darkness of abandonment, it was because, in His love to identify with our cries, He chose to do so.

PSALM 118-21 (119)

"Those who love Your law have great peace; they encounter no stumbling blocks"

After celebrating the Divine Liturgy, it was a certain priest's habit to go to St. Pope Kyrillos VI to take his blessing and ask for his prayers. He would take one of the offertory breads from the Liturgy to him.

On this day, however, the offertory bread was not pleasant in appearance and he assumed that, likewise, it would not be pleasing to the Pope. As he was walking into the entrance of St. Mark's Cathedral, he found holy bread and decided to take a large beautiful one to give to the Saint in place of the offertory bread which he had in his pocket.

He met and greeted the Saint and then gave him the large, beautiful holy bread, and not the bread from the offertory that he had in his pocket. He looked at it from every angle, and turning it over, he sternly looked at the priest and firmly asked, "My son, is this really from the offertory bread?" So he answered him and said, "Forgive me, my master." So, he looked at him even more firmly and said, "My son, hand over the offertory bread!"

He gave it to him with his head bent in great shame wondering what he was going to say upon seeing it. Then, the Saint exclaimed with great joy as he examined the holy bread, "Oh, how sweet and how beautiful!" He continued to say, "Look, my son, how beautiful it is." As he brought the offertory bread closer to the priest's face, he was surprised to see a very clear dark red Cross directly on it and it was very beautiful. The Saint repeated, "Look, my son, how beautiful it is." He answered and said, "Yes, my master, it is beautiful indeed."

On a Culture of Humility

A definition of "culture" includes the customs associated with a particular group or nation. The Church also has a culture and it has nothing to do with language, race or even rituals. It is a "culture of humility" which expresses itself in how the Church worships, along with how we conduct ourselves with one another. The Mother of God is an image of the Church not only in a theological sense, but also in her person as she represents the culture of the Church; she is humble, unassuming, unimposing, and unprovocative. A true monastic community is also representative of this culture.

In the Divine Liturgy, all members worship together in unison, whether in gesture or song, avoiding anything that causes one member to stand out from the rest. We bow together, cross ourselves together, sit and stand at the same time. In this manner we avoid provoking one another to jealousy or distracting another member by our actions and drawing attention to ourselves. In our conversations, we are called to give preference to others, to be unimposing, and to avoid criticism or any hurtful speech. This also means avoiding arguments and disputes. "Where do wars and fights come from among you? Do they not come from your desires for pleasure that war in your members?" (Jas 4:1).

The culture of humility is also one of hiddenness. While some gifts are given by God for the edification of the Church and are, therefore, public gifts, our secret and intimate gifts from God should not be displayed or paraded. We must always remember that the Incarnation took place in silence, as did the birth of the Savior, and even His Resurrection and Ascension are wrapped in silence and humility. A soul that wishes to progress in the interior life must always strive to be hidden. If we desire yet an even more perfect way, we must be hidden from ourselves. That means we must not be overly concerned and preoccupied with ourselves. If we are simple and trusting, even in our own spiritual life we will be less anxious about the condition of our soul and its progress. As one spiritual father said, we should not spy on ourselves.

PSALM 118-22 (119)

"I long for Your salvation, O Lord, and Your law is my delight"

A certain man had a sister who became very ill and suffered more and more as her pregnancy progressed. They took her to the doctor who recommended a specific injection that could help her.

They started to look in every pharmacy in Cairo, until they found someone who said he could have it for them in four hours. The brother suggested that while waiting for the injection, they should go visit St. Pope Kyrillos VI. When they arrived, the Saint was in his cell and they were given permission to go in and see him. The brother started talking and mentioning how his sister was sick, but then they noticed that the Saint was totally absorbed in prayer. After a short while the Saint said, "Everything will be alright, my son, everything will be alright. In two hours your sister will give birth to a baby girl. Put this crucifix around her neck." He then gave him a small Cross and a piece of cotton anointed with holy oil and asked him to anoint the mother and baby with it.

They never went back to the pharmacist. Instead, they went straight to the hospital and his sister had already been taken into the delivery room. After two hours she gave birth, exactly as the blessed St. Pope Kyrillos VI had told them.

On the Second Coming of the Lord

All of our Christian faith is grounded in events. God has always acted in time, and in His Incarnation, has entered directly into human history. In the Nicene Creed we are constantly reminded of the God, "Who created heaven and earth, was incarnate and became man, was crucified, buried, rose from the dead, ascended into the heavens, and is coming again in His glory to judge the living and the dead." We live between the time of the Incarnation and the time of the Second Coming. Christ's return is a part of human history.

In His Second Coming, Christ will not teach, nor will He suffer anything at the hands of man, but He will come "awesome and full of glory" (*Divine Liturgy of St. Basil*) as a Judge. The day of Christ's return is only fearful for the unrepentant sinner or obstinate unbeliever. But for the Christian who lives in hope, the Lord says to us, "look up and lift up your heads, for your redemption draws near" (Lk 21:28). Many Christians, unfortunately, get swept up in dramatic apocalyptic predictions and speculations about the last times. As much as we are called to keep watch over the signs of the times, we also have to "keep watch" over our hearts and any inordinate fears.

On the great day of the Second Coming, everyone will be resurrected. It will be general and simultaneous for both the righteous and sinners, "those who have done good, to the resurrection of life, and those who have done evil, to the resurrection of condemnation" (Jn 5:29). The transformation will encompass not only our bodies, but all the creation (Ro 8:22). This is something to joyfully anticipate, as St. Peter says, "Nevertheless we, according to His promise, look for new heavens and a new earth in which righteousness dwells" (2 Pe 3:7-13). This is the day that all darkness shall flee, all opposition shall vanish, all injustices made right, and every tear wiped away (Re 21:4).

Elder Paisios of Mount Athos was visited in a vision by the martyr St. Euphemia. He asked her how she endured all her tortures. Her response was that if she knew then what she now sees of the glory of the souls that are next to God, she would have requested her martyrdom to last forever.

"Do not love the world, nor things which are in the world. The world shall pass away and all its desires; but he who does the will of God shall abide forever. Amen" (*Divine Liturgy of St. Basil*; 1 Jn 2:17).

Glory to God for all things!

Made in the USA
Las Vegas, NV
30 October 2022

58447837R00136